MUSIC

Curriculum Bank

KEY STAGE TWO
SCOTTISH LEVELS C-E

MUSIC

ELIZABETH ATKINSON AND EMILY FELDBERG

Published by Scholastic Ltd,
Villiers House,
Clarendon Avenue,
Leamington Spa,
Warwickshire CV32 5PR
Text © Elizabeth Atkinson and Emily Feldberg
© 1997 Scholastic Ltd
7 8 9 0   3 4 5

AUTHORS
ELIZABETH ATKINSON AND EMILY FELDBERG

EDITOR
LIBBY RUSSELL

SERIES DESIGNER
LYNNE JOESBURY

DESIGNER
RACHEL WARNER

ILLUSTRATIONS
ANN JOHNS

COVER ILLUSTRATION
JONATHAN BENTLEY

INFORMATION TECHNOLOGY CONSULTANT
MARTIN BLOWS

SCOTTISH 5–14 LINKS
MARGARET SCOTT AND SUSAN GOW

Designed using Aldus Pagemaker
Printed in Great Britain by Bell and Bain Ltd., Glasgow

British Library Cataloguing-in-Publication Data
A catalogue record for this book is available from the
British Library.

ISBN 0-590-53415-7

Contents

Acknowledgement

The publishers gratefully acknowledge permission to reproduce the following copyright material:

Penguin Books Limited for 'Play No Ball' by Gerard Benson from *The Magnificent Callisto* © 1992, Gerard Benson (1992, Blackie Children's Books)

Every effort has been made to trace copyright holders and the publishers apologise for any inadvertent omissions.

Dedication

This book is dedicated to Dick Addison, who convinced so many of us that we could be musicians.

We would like to thank all those who have given us support and encouragement in the writing of this book. From Emily, thanks go to the staff and pupils of Walkergate Junior School, Newcastle upon Tyne and the Primary PGCE students and the teachers on the music GEST course at Newcastle University for being lively critical guinea pigs.

From Elizabeth, thanks go to the Primary BA, BEd and PGCE students at Sunderland University and to her colleagues on the staff for their interest and enthusiasm.

Last but not least, thanks to Emily's mum for finding out ridiculous facts for us at crazy times of the day and night, to Elizabeth's parents for the use of their magnificent computer facilities, and to all three of them for reminding us of the need for sleep!

There is an audio cassette available to accompany this book. It contains a variety of listening selections conveniently collected and professionally-produced on one tape. Each track is directly linked to one or more activities in this book and, together, the pieces cover a range of styles, periods and cultures to support the UK national curricula requirements for music. The Key Stage Two Curriculum Bank Music cassette can be ordered from:

Scholastic Educational Books,
Westfield Road,
Southam,
Warwickshire CV33 0JH.

Please quote ISBN 0 590 53789 X.

Introduction

Scholastic Curriculum Bank is a series for all primary teachers, providing an essential planning tool for devising comprehensive schemes of work as well as an easily accessible and varied bank of practical, classroom-tested activities with photocopiable resources.

Designed to help planning for and implementation of progression, differentiation and assessment, *Scholastic Curriculum Bank* offers a structured range of stimulating activities with clearly stated learning objectives that reflect the programmes of study, and detailed lesson plans that allow busy teachers to put ideas into practice with the minimum amount of preparation time. The photocopiable sheets that accompany many of the activities provide ways of integrating purposeful application of knowledge and skills, differentiation, assessment and record-keeping.

Opportunities for formative assessment are highlighted within the activities where appropriate. Ways of using information technology for different purposes and in different contexts are integrated into the activities where appropriate, and more explicit guidance is provided at the end of the book.

The series covers all the primary curriculum subjects, with separate books for Key Stages 1 and 2 or Scottish Levels A–B and C–E. It can be used as a flexible resource with any scheme, to fulfil National Curriculum and Scottish 5–14 requirements and to provide children with a variety of different learning experiences that will lead to effective acquisition of skills and knowledge.

SCHOLASTIC CURRICULUM BANK MUSIC

Scholastic Curriculum Bank Music enables teachers to plan comprehensive and structured coverage of the primary music curriculum and enables pupils to develop the required skills, knowledge and understanding through carefully planned activities. These activities do not presuppose any particular musical knowledge or experience on the part of either the teacher or the children. There is one book for Key Stage 1/Scottish Levels A–B and one for Key Stage 2/ Scottish Levels C–E.

Bank of activities

This book provides a range of creative music activities designed for the non-specialist teacher working with a whole class.

Accompanying cassette

Many of the activities use recordings of music which are available on a cassette which can be purchased to accompany this book. The extracts are approximately two minutes each. This is so that the children can really listen with concentration to the extract. Any longer and their attention can wander. If you do not have the cassette, you can select your own version of the music or your own music if a particular piece is not needed, using the guidelines given in each activity. The ◇ icon shows which activities use recorded music from the cassette.

Lesson plans

Detailed lesson plans, under clear headings, are given for each activity and provide materials for immediate implementation in the classroom. The structure for each activity is as follows:

Activity title box

The information contained in the box at the beginning of each activity outlines the following key aspects:

▲ *Activity title and learning objective* – For each activity, a clearly-stated learning objective is given in bold italics. These learning objectives break down aspects of the programmes of study into manageable, teaching and learning chunks, and their purpose is to aid planning for progression. These objectives can be easily referenced to the National Curriculum and Scottish 5–14 requirements by using the overview grid at the end of this chapter (pages 9 to 12). (The grid shows key areas of PoS for each activity, but you will find that each activity covers numerous other aspects of the music curriculum.)

▲ *Class organisation/Likely duration* – Icons ✝✝ and ⏰ signpost the suggested group sizes for each activity and the approximate amount of time required to complete it. Some activities are written to cover two or three sessions, while you may choose to extend other activities into more than one session.

▲ *Difficulty* – Icon ♫ denotes the difficulty level of the activity, ranging from easy, through medium, to advanced. Each chapter is arranged progressively, with the easiest activity at the beginning (with the exception of the *Classical music* chapter which is arranged chronologically).

Previous skills/knowledge needed

Information is given here when it is necessary for the children to have acquired specific knowledge or skills prior to carrying out the activity.

Key background information

The information in this section is intended to help the teacher to understand the musical concepts and ideas covered in each activity. It generally goes beyond the level of understanding of most children, but will help to give the teacher confidence to ask and answer questions and to guide the children in their investigations.

Vocabulary

Children and teachers often have difficulty finding suitable words to talk about the music they make or hear. This section gives the key musical vocabulary that occurs naturally in the context of an activity. Some vocabulary may appear very simple at first, but may have a particular meaning or be particularly applicable in a musical context. This is usually explained in the activity.

Introduction

Preparation

This section gives advice on what preparation is needed for the activity. The time required varies from one to fifteen minutes. Preparation may involve listening to a short music extract, making photocopies, finding a working tape recorder, or getting out instruments.

Resources needed

All of the materials needed to carry out the activity are listed, so that either the pupils or the teacher can gather them together easily before the beginning of the teaching session.

What to do

This section gives clear and supportive instructions, including suggestions for questions and discussion as well as highlighting any problems that might arise and suggesting how to solve them.

Suggestion(s) for extension/support

Ideas are given for ways of providing for differentiation where activities lend themselves to this purpose. In all cases, suggestions are provided as to how each activity can be modified for the less able or extended for the more able.

Assessment opportunities

Where appropriate, opportunities for formative assessment of the children's work during or after a specific activity are highlighted.

Opportunities for IT

Where opportunities for IT present themselves, these are briefly outlined with reference to particularly suitable types of program. The chart on page 159 presents specific areas of IT covered in the activities, together with more detailed support on how to apply particular types of program. Selected lesson plans serve as models for other activities by providing more comprehensive guidance on the application of IT, and these are indicated by the bold page numbers on the grid and the ◈ icon at the start of an activity.

Display ideas

Where they are relevant and innovative, display ideas are incorporated into activity plans and illustrated with examples.

Reference to photocopiable sheets

Where activities include photocopiable activity sheets, generally small reproductions of these are included in the lesson plans, together with guidance notes for their use and, where appropriate, suggested answers are provided. However, some sheets are are intended for use with more than one activity, and so to avoid unnecessary repetition, the above does not always apply.

Moving forward

This section gives clear links within and between chapters to enable you to plan for progression and continuity.

Assessment

There are no separate assessment activities in this book as every activity is seen as an assessment opportunity. This is discussed fully in the *Assessment* section at the end of the book. This section gives varied and practical assessment ideas as well as a range of sample recording sheets.

Photocopiable activity sheets

Many of the activities are supported by photocopiable sheets for the teacher or children to use. However, these are only included in an activity where they genuinely support the musical development of the children. Some sheets relate to one activity only, whereas others can be used with several activities. Some of the sheets are primarily for assessment and recording purposes, and can be found in the assessment section near the end of the book.

Cross-curricular links

These are shown on the grid on page 160. The grid shows those aspects of the activities that have a cross-curricular dimension, as well as showing where music might be used to support other curricular areas beyond the specific activities in this book.

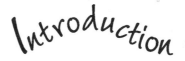

MUSIC AT KEY STAGE 2

This is a book about confidence: teacher confidence and pupil confidence. In spite of the fact that in 1993 OFSTED reported that music was better taught at primary level by specialists and non-specialists alike than many other subjects, it is still the subject that causes the greatest anxiety to many primary teachers.

This book is based on one simple principle:
You don't have to be able to sing, play an instrument or to be a music expert to be a good teacher of music, any more than you have to be a poet or a novelist to be a good teacher of language.

The book hands over the responsibility for primary music from the specialist to the classroom teacher. It is recognised, however, that while the teacher is not expected to be a music expert they can and should have very high expectations of the children. Therefore, while none of these activities are particularly hard to teach, they offer the opportunity to make increasingly challenging demands on the children. The curriculum co-ordinator has a vital role here in supporting what the teacher and children do, but in the final analysis, what happens is up to non-specialist classroom teachers making it work for themselves.

Progression is built into the book in a way that enables you to track your own pathways through the activities, based on your classroom themes and knowledge of the children's musical needs and interests. You might, for example, start with an easy activity in the *Listening* chapter, move on to a more difficult one in *Composing* and then look in depth at one particular style in the *Classical music* chapter. Alternatively, you could start with some simple rhythm activities from *Basic skills*, move on to an exploration of pop music in the *Pop, rock and jazz* chapter, and then investigate West African rhythms in the *World music* chapter. Whichever route you take, you can ensure progression and continuity by referring to the 'Moving forward' section of each activity, and monitor children's progress by taking note of the 'Assessment opportunities'. If you are devising a scheme of work in music for your whole school, you can use these links within and between chapters to tailor your scheme to the particular requirements of each year group, linking music where appropriate with other areas of the curriculum. (The cross-curricular grid on page 160 is designed to help you with this.) If the children have not yet had much experience in the National Curriculum, you can use or adapt activities in the Key Stage 1 *Curriculum Bank: Music* book either alongside or as a preparation for those in this book. The two books have been written together with progression in mind, and the activities at Key Stage 1 develop the skills needed for work at Key Stage 2.

The more experience you gain of these activities, the more confident you are likely to feel, and the more you expect of your pupils, the more they will achieve. Progression in primary music is as much about the growing confidence of the teacher as it is about the increasing skills and knowledge of the children; you may be surprised at how much they can achieve. Progression occurs as much through repeating an activity as through moving on to another one. Take note of the children's increasing knowledge and skills as you work with them through the school year.

Finally, if you find that the children get on particularly well with a certain activity, the whole class can take up the 'Suggestion(s) for extension', or you might prefer to use the activity as a starting point and follow on with your own ideas from there. If you are not sure how to get going, try one of the *Basic Skills* activities or an easy activity from any of the other chapters, and see how it goes. It may not always work – we all have disasters from time to time, but do not be discouraged. The only difference between an experienced and inexperienced music teacher is that the latter is used to picking herself or himself up off the floor after disasters and going back for more.

Learning objective	PoS/AO	Content	Type of activity	Page
Basic skills				
To develop the skill of starting and stopping with increasing accuracy and finesse in response to a conductor.	2a; 4b. **Using materials, techniques, skills and media** – *Using instruments and voice: Level A.*	Stopping and starting at an exact moment in response to hand signals.	Whole class, then groups following conductor's signs; children and teacher conducting.	14
To develop awareness and control of high, medium and low sounds.	2a; 4a. *Using the voice: Level A.*	Using hands, bodies and voices to explore, control and imitate sounds at different pitches.	Whole class exploring voice and body sounds moving in response to sounds.	15
To reinforce the concept of volume and develop skills in voice and/or instrument control in response to a conductor.	2c. *Using instruments and voice: Level A.*	Using instruments or voices to practise both gradual and sudden changes in volume, in response to a conductor.	Whole class then groups playing instruments or singing, conducting and following conductor.	17
To develop awareness of silence in music and introduce the concept of creating sustained silence deliberately.	2b; 4a. **Expressing feelings, ideas, thoughts and solutions** – *Creating and designing: Level A.*	Creating loud sounds with voices, bodies or instruments and contrasting them with periods of silence.	Whole class using voices or instruments, conducting or following.	18
To develop skills in learning and playing rhythms by ear, and keeping a steady pulse.	2b, g. **Using materials...** – *Using instruments: Level A.*	Imitating and repeating rhythmic patterns using body sounds/instruments.	Whole class using body sounds or instruments, teacher- then child-led.	19
To develop skills in controlling tempo (speed) and keeping in time with a changing pulse.	2d; 4a. *Investigating/exploring sound: Level A.*	Responding to and initiating different speeds through movement and body sounds.	Whole class using movement and body sounds, teacher- then child-directed.	21
To develop awareness and control of different types of sound.	2e; 4a. *Using instruments: Level A.*	Exploring different instrument sounds.	Whole class using instruments, investigating and describing.	22
To introduce the concept of scales and give the opportunity to play and work with them.	2a, b; 4a. *As above: Level B.*	Playing simple five-note scales on tuned percussion instruments.	Groups playing instruments and practising skill of playing. Teacher-directed.	23
Composing				
To give experience of composing simple rhythms and melodies using tuned and untuned instruments, and of using informal notation.	2b, f, g; 4a, c; 5b, d. **Expressing feelings...** – *Creating and designing/ Communicating and presenting: Level B.*	Making up three simple melodies and rhythms on tuned/untuned percussion and ordering them with the use of a die. Playing and notating the results.	Whole class then groups, composing, playing, notating within a game.	26
To develop ability to choose instruments and compose with them to create a special effect.	2e, f; 4a, c; 5g; 6f. *As above: Level B.*	Choosing and ordering sounds to represent sounds of the different activities involved in building Hadrian's Wall or a Roman road.	Whole class in groups exploring sounds and composing using instruments and body, notating composition.	28
To develop ability to select and use sounds for composition.	2e; 3a, b; 4a, c; 5f, g, h; 6b. *As above: Level B.*	Using both a painting and a piece of music as a stimulus for improvisation and composition.	Whole class then groups; looking at Impressionist painting then composing, conducting. Taping and evaluating an option.	31

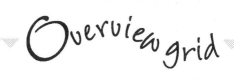
Learning objective	PoS/AO	Content	Type of activity	Page
To develop rhythmic and vocal skills and the ability to keep in time with others.	2b, c; 3b; 4c, d; 5f. *Using materials... – Using the voice/ Communicating and presenting: Level B.*	Using the words and rhythm of a poem to create a performance piece.	Whole class then groups, using voices and body sounds, performing together as a class and in groups. Listening to contemporary Rap.	34
To develop the use of voices as musical instruments and their creative use in composition.	2a, e; 3a, b; 4a, d, e; 5f, g; 6b. *As above: Level B.*	Using voice sounds for improvisation and composition.	Whole class then groups, exploring, experimenting with voice, composing, performing, listening to Tudor music.	37
Listening				
To develop musical vocabulary, musical awareness and the ability to listen purposefully.	4e, f; 6b, c, d, e. *Evaluating and appreciating – Observing, listening, reflecting, describing and responding: Level D.*	Using a range of photocopiable sheets as a focus for listening.	Whole class, groups, individuals; responding to music in a written form, teacher- and child-directed depending on photocopiable sheet used.	40
To develop concentrated listening and the ability to express opinions about a piece of music.	3a, b; 4f; 6e. *As above: Level D.*	Listening five or more times to a piece of music and drawing a line to represent how the music goes up and down.	Whole class working individually using pencil and paper.	42
To develop awareness of mood within music and introduce the concept of representing this in abstract form.	2c, f, g; 3a, b; 4f; 6d. *As above: Level D.*	Listening to a piece of music and responding by compiling a visual representation of it.	Whole class, group or individuals using paper, pencil or paint.	44
To develop the ability to distinguish between different musical styles.	3a, b; 4e; 6c, d, e. *As above: Level D.*	Listening to several pieces of music and identifying the differences between them.	Whole class, teacher-directed, listening, discussing.	46
To develop awareness of structure and texture in music.	2e, f, g; 3a, b; 6b, d, e. *As above: Level D.*	Representing structure and texture of the music that is being listened to in collage work.	Whole class, group or individuals using art materials in collage work.	48
Classical music				
To develop awareness of the style of Tudor music.	2a, b; 3b; 4b, e; 5d; 6c. *Evaluating and appreciating – Observing, listening...: Level D.*	Listening to a Tudor song, composing a new verse and an instrumental accompaniment.	Whole class then groups listening, making up words, composing, playing. Teacher/child-directed.	52
To introduce the principal features of Baroque music and to develop listening skills.	2d, f; 3a; 4e, f; 6d, e. *As above: Level D.*	Listening to music by Bach, imitating the instruments, analysing the instrumentation using a chart.	Whole class working in two groups, then filling in charts. Teacher-directed.	56
To develop awareness of the style of Mozart and the concept of arpeggios.	2a, b, g; 3a, b; 4a, e; 5h; 6c. *Using materials... – Using instruments: Level D.*	Using arpeggios played on instruments to compose music similar in style to that of Mozart. Using these compositions as a basis for listening to Mozart's music.	Whole class then groups learning a skill composing using notation while listening to Mozart.	59

Learning objective	PoS/AO	Content	Type of activity	Page
To develop awareness of the narrative use of music and of different musical styles and techniques.	2c–e, f; 3a; 4f; 6b, c, e. *Evaluating and appreciating – Observing, listening..: Level D.*	Listening to, comparing, discussing and writing ballet music.	Whole class in pairs, listening to music, discussing and writing opinions.	62
To introduce and experience the style of waltz music.	2a, b, f, g; 4a, b; 5b, e, f; 6c. *As above: Level D.*	Playing a Victorian-style waltz using xylophones and other percussion.	Whole class playing instruments, using chords, performing waltzes, improvising, reading simple notation.	65
To develop awareness of contemporary experimental music through listening and composition.	2a, b, g; 3b; 4a, b; 5b, d; 6b. *As above: Level D.*	Rhythmic improvisation with hands, voices and bodies, then rhythmic improvisation and composition with instruments, using music by John Cage as a stimulus.	Whole class, then groups improvising, listening, composing and playing. Teacher/child-directed.	68
World music				
To introduce some of the main features of Arabic music.	2b; 3a, b; 4a, e; 5e; 6c, e. *As above: Level D.*	Working with a modern setting of an Arabic traditional tune and comparing it with Western modern music.	Whole class playing drum rhythms listening to Arabic music, describing music and respond to it.	74
To introduce Western European folk music and develop awareness of its structure through movement.	2b, d, g; 3a; 4d, e; 6c, d. *As above: Level D.*	Listening to Northumbrian folk music and devising simple dance steps to go with it.	Whole class, teacher-directed, then small groups, child-directed. Making up dances in response to music.	76
To introduce the Chinese style of music.	2a, e, f; 3a; 4a, e; 5f; 6b. *Using materials... – Using instruments: Level D.*	Using intervals, fourths and specific instruments to compose music which gives a Chinese-style sound.	Groups using instruments, practising, teacher-directed, composing, child-directed. Listening to Chinese traditional music.	78
To develop awareness of African rhythms and give experience of complex rhythms.	2b, f; 3a; 4b; 5c, h; 6e. *As above: Level D.*	Simultaneously playing rhythms which have contrasting emphasis to create complex rhythms, listening to African drumming.	Whole class, teacher-directed, using body sounds, optional instruments, listening to African drumming.	80
To develop awareness of the music of South-East Asia and the use of a similar style in composition.	2g; 3a; 4b, e; 5c, h; 6a. *As above: Level D.*	Listening to music from Thailand and composing a piece in a similar style.	Whole class, then groups, listening, composing and performing. Teacher/child-directed.	83
To familiarise children with the sound and structure of Indian ragas.	2a, e; 3a; 4e; 5e, f; 6b, c. *Using materials... – Using instruments: Level D.*	Listening to, analysing and playing an Indian raga.	Groups, listening to, analysing, talking about Indian classical music; exploring instruments, composing.	86
Pop, rock and jazz				
To develop ability to listen analytically to familiar pop music and develop understanding of it.	2b; 3a, b; 4f; 6b, c, e. *Evaluating and appreciating – Observing, listening..: Level D.*	Listening to and describing favourite songs.	Pairs then whole class, using cassette player, child-directed; presenting written and spoken opinion to class.	92

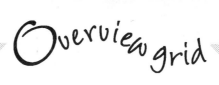

Learning objective	PoS/AO	Content	Type of activity	Page
To build on and develop the children's awareness of popular song structure through composition.	2g; 4b; 5a, d, f; 6f. *Expressing feelings... – Creating and designing/ Communicating and presenting: Level D.*	Making up and performing a pop song.	Small groups working independently, using instruments and simple notations, performing and recording the results.	94
To develop awareness of musical structure through listening to jazz.	2f, g; 4e; 6a, e. *Evaluating and appreciating – Observing, listening...: Level D.*	Using a chart to analyse the structure of a piece of recorded jazz music.	Whole class listening, discussing and writing results on paper.	96
To develop awareness of song structure in jazz and pop music, and enhance compositional skills.	2g; 4a; 5a, e; 4e, f. *Expressing feelings... – Creating and designing/ Communicating and presenting: Level D.*	Composing and performing a new middle section for a song.	Whole class then individuals, pairs or groups, composing with instruments or voices, child-directed.	98
To develop rhythmic skills and awareness of complex rhythmic patterns and promote performance skills.	2b, e, g; 3a; 4b, c; 5e; 6c. *As above: Level D.*	Finding and using everyday objects to create a complex rhythm by combining simple ones.	Whole class using instruments from environment, teacher/ child-directed, performing resulting piece.	101
Notation				
To introduce and use the concept of colour as a form of notation.	2a; 4a; 5b, f. *Expressing feelings... – Creating and designing: Level D.*	Using colour coding on tuned instruments to denote notes which should be played. Reading the notated melody as a class, then working to compose and notate own tunes.	Whole class in groups using instruments, child-directed.	104
To develop reading and devising of complex notation using a grid.	2b; 4a; 5b, c, h. *As above: Level D.*	Working with a four-way grid, playing simple rhythms from notation, developing idea of playing four rhythms at the same time using the notation on the grid.	Whole class then groups, teacher- then child-directed, using body sounds or instruments following and writing grid notation.	106
To develop the concept of graphic notation and use it as a form of composing.	2f; 4d; 5b, h. *As above: Level D.*	Introducing graphic notation and using it to make an instant composition. Developing the idea to notate more than one instrument playing at the same time.	Whole class, then groups, teacher- then child-directed, using a range of writing materials.	108
To introduce the concept of time value (the length of notes) in formal notation.	2b, g; 5b. *As above: Level B.*	Learning the notation for different lengths of notes and using this to count sets of beats.	Whole class, groups and individuals, teacher- then child-directed, using pencil and paper, reading notation.	110
To introduce the principle of pitch notation (writing down specific notes) and to develop awareness of the way musical phrases can be combined to make a tune.	2b, g; 5b; 6d, e. *As above: Level D.*	Rearranging sections of a familiar tune in order to create and play new ones.	Whole class then groups, child-directed, using voices or instruments, reading notation.	114

Entries given in italics relate to the Scottish 5–14 Guidelines for Expressive Arts.

MUSIC

Basic Skills

This chapter provides the building blocks needed for all the activities in this book. It also introduces the elements of music as identified in the National Curriculum: pitch, duration, dynamics, tempo, timbre and texture. All the activities follow on from the basic skills developed in the *Curriculum Bank: Music* Key Stage 1 book: if your children are relatively inexperienced in music, some of the Key Stage 1 activities could be used.

The activities here can be used in a number of ways:
▲ as a starting-point from which the children's learning can be taken in any direction chosen;
▲ as self-contained music sessions;
▲ as warm-ups to longer sessions (they provide an ideal introduction to any music session, particularly if the one chosen is related to the theme of the session);
▲ as a preparation for activities in other chapters.

There are three important points to remember:
▲ Skills will develop the more often they are practised.
▲ The more ways in which skills are used, the freer children will feel to use them in their compositions and performances.
▲ The more times skills are revisited, the greater the learning value will be: these are not one-offs to do just once, then move on – they are the backbone of children's musical experience.

However, skills alone do not make a curriculum. Music is about more than this: it is about creativity, imagination and enjoyment. The skills developed here need to be *used* in order to be worthwhile.

STOP AND START

To develop the skill of starting and stopping with increasing accuracy and finesse in response to a conductor.

†† *Whole class, then groups of four to five.*

🕐 *10–15 minutes.*

♫ *Easy.*

Previous skills/knowledge needed

By the beginning of Key Stage 2, children should have some experience of starting and stopping in response to a signal and be ready to refine their responses as in this activity. If they are still very inexperienced, you could try the activities in the *Basic skills* chapter of the Key Stage 1 book before doing this one. You might also find it useful to refer to photocopiable sheet 122 – 'The language of conducting', for a range of signals that could be used.

Key background information

The beginning and end of any piece of music is always important; the beginning sets the standard and mood of what is going to happen, and the end leaves a final impression. A single note on a triangle can be transformed from a miserable, tentative ping to an atmospheric and exciting introduction to a piece of music through the use of a convincing start. Starting together can be hard for children (and teachers) but it is well worth the extra practice since the benefit will be felt throughout the children's music-making. A convincing start also gives the message that this music is to be taken seriously.

Vocabulary

Start, stop, beginning, ending.

Preparation

If you would prefer to use instruments (tuned and untuned), gather enough for each child to have one of their own.

Resources needed

Optional: tuned and untuned instruments (see 'Preparation').

What to do

Explain to the children that they are going to learn how to start and stop so that everyone is doing it at exactly the same time. Ask them to count '1, 2, 3, start' with you a few times. When they are confident with this, put in a clap (or a sound from the instruments) instead of, or as well as, 'start'. Have high standards: ask the children to really concentrate on it so that the start sounds like one sound.

Now discuss what sort of signal might be suitable for a *starting sign*. First this will be used in conjunction with the '1, 2, 3, start', but as the children gain experience and confidence, the hand signal should become the only sign, with '1, 2, 3' being mouthed silently. The movement you choose needs to be big, so that everyone can see it, simple so that everyone can understand it and quick so that everyone starts or stops playing at the same time. A vertical downward movement of the hand is a good signal (see photocopiable sheet 122 for more ideas). When you have agreed on a starting sign discuss a *stopping sign*. Again this needs to be big, simple and quick. When both signals have been decided, try them out.

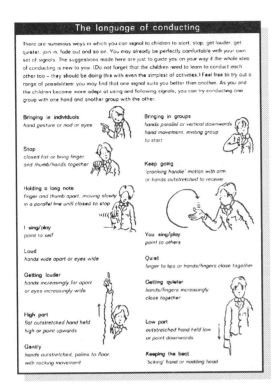

The language of conducting

There are numerous ways in which you can signal to children to start, stop, get louder, get quieter, join in, fade out and so on. You may already be perfectly comfortable with your own set of signals. The suggestions made here are just to guide you on your way if the whole idea of conducting is new to you. (Do not forget that the children need to learn to conduct each other too – they should be doing this with even the simplest of activities.) Feel free to try out a range of possibilities: you may find that one signal suits you better than another. As you and the children become more adept at using and following signals, you can try conducting one group with one hand and another group with the other.

Bringing in individuals
hand gesture or nod or eyes

Stop
closed fist or bring finger and thumb/hands together

Holding a long note
finger and thumb apart, moving slowly in a parallel line until closed to stop

I sing/play
point to self

Loud
hands wide apart or eyes wide

Getting louder
hands increasingly far apart or eyes increasingly wide

High part
flat outstretched hand held high or point upwards

Gently
hands outstretched, palms to floor, with rocking movement

Bringing in groups
hands parallel or vertical downwards hand movement, inviting group to start

Keep going
'cranking handle' motion with arm or hands outstretched to receive

You sing/play
point to others

Quiet
finger to lips or hands/fingers close together

Getting quieter
hands/fingers increasingly close together

Low part
outstretched hand held low or point downwards

Keeping the beat
'ticking' hand or nodding head

Ask the children to sit where they can see your hands (or whatever part of you is going to make the signals). When the starting sign is made they are going to make the loudest (or softest) noise they can. Remind them that they will have to be facing you so that they can see the signals.

Start the children off and after about 15 seconds make the stopping sign. There will always be one or two children who do not get it the first time. Make the activity into a game and try it three or four times. Expect that the children will be able to do it with practice.

When the children are responding confidently and accurately to the signals, split the class into groups and ask individuals to take it in turns to be the conductor while the others respond.

Suggestion(s) for extension
Children who are responding well can experiment with starting at a given volume (either loud or quiet) each time, indicated by the conductor using hand signals.

Suggestion(s) for support
If the children are having difficulty, go back over the '1, 2, 3, start' and give them more practice.

Assessment opportunities
This activity gives opportunities to assess children's ability to start and stop with increasing accuracy in response to a conductor, and to act as conductors themselves.

Moving forward
The skills developed here will prepare the children for the performing involved in many of the activities in this book, and will help them to perform their own compositions with appropriate skill and finesse.

CONTROLLING PITCH

To develop awareness and control of high, medium and low sounds.

†† *Whole class.*

🕒 *5–10 minutes.*

♫ *Easy.*

Key background information
By the beginning of Key Stage 2, children generally have a fairly good awareness of pitch and of the way in which the terms 'high' and 'low' relate to musical sounds. In order to make full use of this awareness, it is necessary for them to have confidence in controlling pitch themselves. This activity is aimed at developing that confidence through the use of voices, reinforced by hand and body movements. It will help them both to control the pitch of their own voices and to match them to the pitch of others. It will also provide valuable aural awareness which will help the children to make good use of pitch control when they are playing instruments. (This activity could be repeated with instruments, following the same steps but excluding the hand and body movements.)

Vocabulary
High, medium, low, pitch.

Preparation
Make a space available where all the children can stand in a circle, with room to stretch their arms out sideways.

What to do
Start with all the children standing in a circle. Ask them to use their voices to make the highest sound they possibly can, then the lowest sound, then one somewhere in the middle. They can squeak, growl, hum or sing these sounds – it is the pitch, not the type of sound, that is important. Repeat this a few times until everyone is concentrating and responding well.

Now ask the children to use their hands and bodies to indicate the pitch of the sounds as they make them, standing on their toes and reaching high for the highest sounds, crouching down and touching the floor for the lowest sounds, and reaching sideways to their neighbours' shoulders for those in between. Use these movements yourself to conduct the sounds, rather than giving verbal instructions, this will ensure that the children are responding to your signals as a conductor. Do this a few times, then invite individual children to take turns as the conductor.

Standing in the circle yourself, start a 'Mexican wave' of sound round the circle. To do this, make a single voice sound (with the appropriate movement) which is copied by your neighbour, then by their neighbour and so on, until the sound (and movement) return to you, and you start again with a new one. Ask the children to copy their neighbour's pitch as closely as they can, as this will help to develop fine control of the pitch of their voice. (It will help if they also copy the *type* of sound, rather than trying to produce a different sound at the same pitch.) Again, hand over control to them once they have got used to the idea, by asking different children to start off new 'sound waves'.

Finally, start a steady clap (on your own) of 1 – 2 – 3 – 4 1 – 2 – 3 – 4 and ask the children to make their own series of sounds in time with the beat. They can make sounds at any number of different pitches, as long as they use an appropriate movement to go with each. The result will be a surprisingly complex improvisation in sound and movement.

Suggestion(s) for extension

Children who find this type of pitch differentiation very easy can explore more subtle differences in pitch within a single range (high, medium or low), using smaller differences in hand and body movements to indicate the smaller changes in pitch. They can also work in pairs, either copying each others' sounds and movements or playing a game of opposites, where a high sound is echoed by a low one and vice versa.

Suggestion(s) for support

Some children will have difficulty using the extremes of their vocal range. It will help them if you continue the first part of

the activity for some time (that is, making sounds without movements) until they are more confident. Others may find it hard to co-ordinate their movements with their voices. It will help if they are positioned next to more confident children in the circle, so that they can move along with their neighbour's movements, while imitating their sounds.

Assessment opportunities

As well as monitoring the children's awareness and control of pitch, this activity will enable you to assess their ability to follow visual signals and to create their own sequence of sounds and movements.

Moving forward

This activity links particularly well to 'Musical printout' on page 42, where high and low pitch can be represented by a printout on paper. It also provides essential skills for many of the activities in the *Composing* chapter, particularly 'Composing with voices' on page 37, where children manipulate their own voice sounds to create a vocal composition.

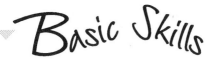

CONTROLLING VOLUME

To reinforce the concept of volume and develop skills in voice and/or instrument control in response to a conductor.

†† *Whole class, then groups of four or five.*

🕐 *10 minutes.*

🎵 *Easy.*

Previous skills/knowledge needed
The children need to have some experience of handling instruments and responding to a conductor. The 'Stop and start' activity in this chapter would be useful for this.

Key background information
Volume, or dynamics, forms a major element of all music, giving each piece its own character or atmosphere. To be able to create loud and soft sounds within either composition or performance is an essential skill.

Vocabulary
Loud , soft, quiet, getting louder (crescendo), getting softer (diminuendo), volume, dynamics.

Preparation
If you prefer to use instruments, provide one for each child. Tuned/untuned percussion or other instruments would all be appropriate for this activity. You may find it useful to refer to 'The language of conducting' photocopiable sheet on page 122 for signals related to volume control.

Resources needed
Optional: tuned/untuned percussion (or other) instruments.

What to do
Explain to the children that you are going to be working with volume, or loud and soft sound. Ask them to make the softest sound they can on their instrument, or with their voice. Listen and tell them that now you want them to make *half as much* noise as that. When they have done this two or three times introduce conducting signs for volume. Put your hands facing palm to palm in front of you, when your hands are almost touching, this indicates a very quiet sound, as your hands move further apart, the volume increases until your arms are at full stretch, indicating the loudest sound the children can make.

Try out loud and quiet sounds with voices or instruments and see how quickly the children can react to the signals. Now tell them that you are going to try and trick them. Starting with your hands about 30cm apart, move them outwards (to indicate an increase in volume), then suddenly move back to the middle position. To start with, the children will be tricked and carry on getting louder even when you have moved your hands back. Continue this until you feel

that they are confident, then introduce another trick, by sometimes moving your hands gradually and sometimes moving them very suddenly. Draw the children's attention to the care needed in controlling their instruments to ensure that they always produce the right volume of sound. When you have practised a few times, ask some of the children to take turns as conductors and see how successfully the rest of the class can follow them. When the children are responding confidently to the signals, ask them to get into groups of four or five and take it in turns to conduct each other.

Suggestion(s) for extension
Children who have worked well in this activity can make up their own 'loud and soft' mini-composition using the signals they have learned.

Suggestion(s) for support
If some children find this activity hard, work with them at making loud and soft sounds and give them plenty of opportunities to practise.

Assessment opportunities
In this activity there are opportunities to assess the children's awareness of volume, their ability to control instruments and their skills in responding to a conductor and acting as conductors themselves.

Moving forward
The children will be able to incorporate the skills they have learned here into their own compositions and performances, using an awareness of dynamics to enhance their music-making.

CREATING SILENCE

To develop awareness of silence in music and introduce the concept of creating sustained silence deliberately.

♦♦ *Whole class.*

⏱ *5 minutes.*

♪ *Easy.*

Previous skills/knowledge needed

The children need to have some experience of handling and controlling instruments and responding to a conductor. The activities 'Stop and start' and 'Controlling volume' in this chapter would both be useful for this.

Key background information

Silence is one of the most powerful tools in music. It can create emotions of fear, sadness, excitement or happiness. It can re-engage a flagging audience and have them sitting on the edge of their seats. Children enjoy making and playing silence, but it does have to be taught. This activity works equally well with instruments, voices or body sounds.

Vocabulary

Silence, pause, rest, pulse, beat.

Preparation

You will need to assemble tuned or untuned instruments for each child if you intend to use them. You might find it useful to look at 'The language of conducting' photocopiable sheet on page 122 for ideas for signals.

Resources needed

Optional: tuned and/or untuned instruments.

What to do

Explain to the children that you are going to be working on the idea of silence, and tell them that it will be a very noisy lesson. Ask them to sit down in silence. Remind them that silence is silence of the body, mouth and instrument. This means that a real silence has no rustles of clothing or scraping of feet. Tell them that you are going to practise making a tiny noise and then being silent again. Ask them all to rub their hands or their knees, something which makes a soft sound. Use a signal to stop the sound – this could be a hand signal or mouthing at them to stop. Encourage them to really listen to the silence as they stop the hand rubbing.

If you are using instruments, give one out to each child and ask them to build up gradually to the loudest noise that they can. Make sure the whole class is watching you before you conduct the stopping sign. The silence effect depends on the children's ability to stop immediately and to keep their instruments absolutely still once the sign has been given. If some children did not see the signal the first time, make a

game of it. Tell them that you will be looking out for the child who does not see the conductor.

When the children have gained their confidence, tell them that this time they are going to play really loudly and when the stopping sign is made they are going to count silently to four in their heads. Before you start playing, practise counting the four silent beats by mouthing one, two, three, four, with the children. This means that they will have to look at the conductor to find out when to start and stop.

Start the children playing loudly and increase the volume even further. When the sound is at it loudest point, make the stop sign. Count slowly up to four in your head, mouthing the count so that the children can see you, then start them off again. Repeat this several times, and on the final time, hold the silence again for a count of four before asking the children to put down their instruments. Ask them if they feel there is real silence, and talk about the effect it has on people listening to it.

The counted out silence can be very effective, as the audience is kept in suspense waiting, partly thinking that the musicians will start playing again and partly wondering if they actually have stopped.

Suggestion(s) for extension
If the children find this activity easy ask them to conduct their own silences and playing time.

Suggestion(s) for support
If some children find it difficult to be silent in response to your signal, make a point of attracting their attention at the vital moment. It is also useful to ask these children to conduct a silence to increase their confidence and involvement in the activity.

Assessment opportunities
This activity gives opportunities to assess the children's awareness of silence as a concept and as a musical tool, and their ability to respond to a conductor's signals.

Moving forward
Once the children have grasped the power and importance of silence, they will be able to make use of it as a musical tool, both in composition and performance.

COPY AND ECHO
To develop skills in learning and playing rhythms by ear, and keeping a steady pulse.
†† *Whole class.*
🕐 *5–10 minutes.*
♫ *Easy.*

Previous skills/knowledge needed
If you are going to use instruments, it will help if the children have had some experience of handling and controlling them, though this activity can also be used to develop these skills.

Key background information
Repetition is an important feature of many styles of music. It is one of the most frequently-used forms of structure in African and Latin American music, for example, and is used widely in Western classical and folk music, where both rhythmic and melodic patterns (tunes) may be repeated. This activity also focuses on the skills of keeping a steady beat and keeping a rhythm going without a pause – two skills which are of crucial importance in playing and performing.

Vocabulary
Echo, copy, imitate, repeat, rhythm, rhythmic, melodic.

Preparation
If you wish to use instruments for this activity, you will need to collect enough for each child to have one.

Resources needed
Optional: tuned or untuned instruments.

What to do
Explain to the children that you want them to copy the rhythmic pattern that you are about to play. Start the activity by lightly slapping your knees or thighs four times in a steady beat, or tapping four beats on an instrument. (Remember that you are only focusing on rhythm here, so even if the children are using instruments, they do not need to play a tune.) Ask the whole class to copy your rhythm, keeping a steady pulse at all times, so that there is no pause between the end of your four beats and the beginning of theirs:

Teacher				Children				Teacher			
○	○	○	○	●	●	●	●	○	○	○	○

Repeat this without stopping until the children are copying confidently, then ask individual children to take it in turns to copy your pattern. Once they are keeping in time, and listening and imitating without a pause, you can gradually introduce new rhythms, still keeping to a count of four, but creating more complex patterns within the four beats.
For example:

Teacher					Children					Teacher			
○	○ ○ ○	○			●	● ● ●		●		○	○ ○ ○	○

If you find it hard to think up new patterns, try saying rhythmic phrases in your head. For example:

Teacher
Ap - ple pear ba - na - - na
○ ○ ○ ○ ○ ○

Children
Ap - ple pear ba - na - - na   **or**
● ● ● ● ● ●

Teacher
Who's a pre - tty po - lly then?
○ ○ ○ ○ ○ ○

Children
Who's a pre - tty po - lly then?
● ● ● ● ● ●

Continue to introduce new rhythms and gradually extend the range of sounds that you are making by using different parts of the body, or playing the instruments in different ways (for example, by striking both the skin and the side of a drum). As they grow more confident, ask the children to make up their own rhythms for the rest of the class to imitate (using words too, if it helps them think of patterns).

Suggestion(s) for extension
For children who find this activity easy, you can make the rhythms more complicated, using a rhythm that lasts for eight beats rather than four. They could try playing a similar game repeating simple melodic rather than rhythmic patterns, such as simple three- or four-note tunes.

Suggestion(s) for support
If some children are finding this activity difficult, simplify the pattern that you are playing, or continue to play the rhythm and wait for their response, giving lots of positive encouragement. You can gradually move towards repeating the patterns without a pause once their confidence has been established.

Assessment opportunities
This activity gives you the opportunity to observe the children's ability to remember and repeat simple rhythms, and to create rhythmic patterns of their own. It also shows their ability to keep a steady beat and to keep a rhythm going without pausing.

Moving forward
The rhythmic awareness and skills developed here can be put to use in all the children's composing and performing work, as well as making them aware of the rhythmic patterns in the music they hear. 'Copy and echo' is a particularly useful technique for composing, as it introduces a feeling of structure into the simplest of pieces.

CONTROLLING TEMPO

To develop skills in controlling tempo (speed) and keeping in time with a changing pulse.

♯♯ *Whole class.*

🕐 *10 minutes.*

♫ *Easy.*

Previous skills/knowledge needed

Rhythmic work such as in the activity 'Copy and echo' in this chapter will be useful.

Key background information

Tempo (or speed) is a very important component of music. The speed of the music can strongly influence the mood of the listeners. When children first start to work with tempo they often have a tendency to get louder as they get faster. As part of the realisation of what tempo is, it is important to try and work against this by using *fast and quiet* as well as *slow and loud* playing.

Vocabulary

Tempo, fast, slow, walking pace, running pace.

What to do

Explain to the children that they are going to be keeping a steady pulse and that the aim is to keep the same speed. Ask them to stand and keep a steady relaxed walk on the spot. Start the walking on the spot yourself to indicate the speed that you want. The children often naturally go faster and faster. If this happens remind them not to go faster but to relax into the pulse, and watch your steady walking on the spot. They have to go at exactly the same speed as you. If they find this difficult, stop briefly and start the pulse going again. How easy they find this will depend on previous musical experience that they have had.

When a pulse is established ask them to stop moving their feet and instead to start tapping three fingers on the palm of their hand, keeping the time of the pulse. (Three fingers are always better than two as it avoids the distraction of raucous giggles when one child realises that they could use two fingers to make a rude sign!) The speed should still be the same as it was when you started. Stop the children briefly and say that now you are going to vary the pace, sometimes it will be faster than before and sometimes slower, but they have to follow you and you are going to try and catch them out.

Start off again with the same steady pulse, again tapped with three fingers on the palm, or a light slap on the knees or thighs. As soon as they become used to the pulse again, make it a bit faster. You need to go fast enough for the children to notice but not so fast that they go out of musical control. Continue this activity by varying your speed. Each time, wait long enough for the majority of the class to have caught on to the new pulse. When the class understands the game, ask a child to be the leader and to change the speed for the group.

Suggestion(s) for extension

If there are children who find this easy, ask them to take control and change the tempo after every 16 beats, making a continuously changing pattern.

Suggestion(s) for support

If children are finding this difficult, ask them to stand next to you and, as the rest of the class are keeping the pulse, lightly tap the speed of the pulse on the palm of their hand, or on their shoulder.

Assessment opportunities

This activity gives the opportunity to assess whether a child is aware that the tempo of music can change, and whether they can control their own tempo and keep in time with a changing pulse.

Moving forward

You can repeat this activity using instruments, either combining moving and playing, or just playing at different speeds. Children can make use of what they have learned here by looking out for changes in tempo in any music that they sing, dance or play, and by incorporating deliberate changes in tempo into their own compositions.

CONTROLLING TIMBRE

To develop awareness and control of different types of sound.

†† *Whole class.*

♩ *10 minutes.*

♫ *Easy.*

Previous skills/knowledge needed

It will help if the children have some experience in controlling instruments and in responding to a conductor. The activities 'Stop and start', 'Controlling volume' (with instruments) and 'Creating silence' in this chapter would all be useful for this.

Key background information

Timbre is the musical term for type or quality of sound. It is the clashing of a cymbal, for example, or the rattle of a tambourine. It can describe the smoothness of notes played on a flute or the rat-a-tat-tat of a snare drum. The timbre of voices can be harsh or mellow, strident or gentle. These qualities are often combined with particular features of rhythm and/or tempo to make up the individual character of a piece of music, and it is sometimes difficult to know whether what we are describing is just one of these elements, or a combination of several.

This activity invites children to focus on timbre through the exploration of instrumental sounds. It can be repeated very successfully with voices or body sounds (clapping, stamping, rubbing hands, clicking teeth), enabling the children to investigate the wide range of sounds they can make without any instruments at all.

The activity uses *volume* as a way of *focusing* on timbre – it is often not until children are playing really quietly that they actually listen to the sounds they are making. It needs to be remembered, however, that the main focus here is on the sounds themselves, not on the volume at which they are played.

Vocabulary

Timbre, rattling, scraping, rough, gentle, tapping, jingling and so on.

Preparation

Have enough instruments ready for the whole class to play. It is a good idea for children who are having instrumental lessons to discover the wide range of sounds their instruments are capable of producing. You might, therefore, invite them to bring their instruments to this session.

Resources needed

Tuned and untuned percussion instruments, plus any other instruments you wish to use.

What to do

Stand the children in a circle, with an instrument each; distribute the instruments to players in such a way that instruments of the same type are *not* next to each other. Point to one child in the circle and ask that child to start playing their instrument in any way they like and to continue playing until you point to them again. Now indicate to their neighbour to start playing as well, then the next child and the next, until everyone in the circle is playing at the same time. When you reach the first child again, signal them to stop, and continue to stop each child in turn until you return to silence.

Ask one or two children to describe and demonstrate how they made their chosen sound. Now ask them to repeat their sounds in a circle, until your hand passes them, when they have to change to a new type of sound. Go round the circle three or four times in this way, exploring different sounds each time.

Now ask everyone to choose a really quiet sound. Go round the circle once like this, then ask for a different sound which is even quieter. Do the same again, once or twice, until the children are really listening to the sounds.

While they are still playing very quietly, ask the children to listen carefully to the sounds around them and to move, still playing, to a position next to someone whose instrument is making a sound similar to their own. Tell them to pay attention to the *sound* they are making, not just the type of instrument they are playing – an instrument might belong in two or more groups, depending upon the way in which it is played. Then ask those who have joined together to move, still playing, towards other instruments with a similar timbre.

Finally, stop the children, discuss their sounds briefly (were they harsh or gentle, rattling or jingling, scraping or tapping sounds) then ask them to play round the circle again, but this time in the sound groups they have created. Conduct the sounds with pointing as before, or choose a child to do so, but this time conduct a whole group in at a time. Finish as you started, with the sounds building up then gradually dying down to nothing as you signal to each group to stop.

INTRODUCING SCALES

To introduce the concept of scales and give children the opportunity to play and work with them.

♯♯ *Whole class in groups of five or six.*

🕐 *15–20 minutes.*

🎵 *Easy.*

Previous skills/knowledge needed
It will help if the children have some experience of playing instruments and listening to the sounds they make. The activity 'Controlling timbre' in this chapter would be particularly useful for this.

Key background information
A scale is a series of notes which are played in a particular order, ascending or descending (or both). Scales are sometimes referred to as 'musical steps'. The *diatonic* scale forms the basis of most Western folk and classical music: this is the scale you hear if you play the consecutive white notes on a keyboard or piano starting at C. You may be familiar with this scale from the song 'Doh, a deer' from the film soundtrack of *The Sound of Music*. Other cultures use other scales: for example the *pentatonic* scale which can be represented by the notes C, D, E, G, A and is common in the music of South-East Asia. Certain scales are characteristic of particular styles of music: for example, many jazz pieces use a *blues* scale which makes them sound quite different from classical or folk tunes. This activity makes use of a simplified version of the diatonic scale, which children can then use as a basis for their own compositions.

Vocabulary
Scale, notes, beat, diatonic, pentatonic, blues scale.

Preparation
If you are not particularly familiar with the idea of scales, try this activity yourself before doing it with the children. If you have a recording of 'Doh, a deer' you may like to listen to it to familiarise yourself with the sequence of notes, you can also use it to introduce the activity to the children (see 'What to do'). Get the instruments ready (see 'Resources needed') in an area large enough for the children to sit round the instruments in groups of four, five or six (depending on the number of instruments available and the number of children in your class).

Resources needed
One xylophone, metallophone, glockenspiel or set of chime bars for each group of four to six children – you will need the notes C, D, E, F and G (all white notes if you are using chime bars) and two beaters for each group. Optional: recording of 'Doh, a deer'.

Suggestion(s) for extension
Children who show that they can create and distinguish sounds with ease can find out how many different sounds they can make with a single instrument. You could also ask them to classify instruments according to timbre, using both classroom instruments and recordings.

Suggestion(s) for support
Some children will need encouragement to play instruments in unconventional ways. If a child is only hitting or shaking an instrument, for example, ask her or him to try rubbing her or his hands across it, blowing onto it, or contrasting the sounds made with tight and loose holds.

Children who find it difficult to listen to each other's sounds will benefit from focusing on extreme contrasts: a rattle versus a continuous note, for example, or an echoing chime bar versus a single sound on the wood block.

Assessment opportunities
This activity provides opportunities to monitor children's ability to control the timbre (sound quality) of instruments, to listen carefully and to use an appropriate vocabulary to describe what they hear.

Moving forward
This activity links particularly well with 'Talking about music' on page 40 which includes a music vocabulary photocopiable sheet for timbre. 'Telling tales: music for ballet' on page 62 invites children to analyse the ways in which composers use timbre to create particular effects. Also, several other activities in the *Composing* chapter rely on the selection and use of appropriate sounds for composition, particularly 'Roman sound picture' on page 28 and 'Pavement café' on page 31.

What to do

Seat the children in groups around the instruments. Either start the activity by playing them a recording of 'Doh a deer' from *The Sound of Music*, or simply play them a scale on one of the instruments, starting on C:

Going up:

C D E F G A B C

Coming down:

C B A G F E D C

Ask the children to sing along by 'lahing' as you play, and try doing the same yourself. Introduce the term 'scale' and explain that this is one of many types of scales used in music throughout the world, and that this is the one the children will be most familiar with, as it is the basis for most of the music they hear. Ask one child in each group to pick up a beater and play the first five notes of the scale: C D E F G. Ask the next person in each group to have the second beater ready so that they can play as soon as the first person has finished, and so on round the group (the first person passes their beater to the third, the second to the fourth and so on). It will help the children to get a sense of the pattern if they play the five notes evenly, keeping a steady beat throughout and counting in sets of four:

Child 1	C D E F G (2 3 4)
Child 2	C D E F G (2 3 4)
Child 3	C D E F G and so on.

Tell the children that they can choose whether they play *up* the five-note scale (starting at C) or *down* it (starting at G). Give them five minutes or so to practise, stressing the importance of keeping a steady beat and listening to each other, then bring the groups together and finish with a grand performance, with all the number ones playing together, then all the number twos, and so on until every member of each group has played.

Suggestion(s) for extension

Children who have coped well with the five-note scale can explore the full range of eight notes:

C D E F G A B C.

Alternatively, they can experiment with rearranging the notes in an order of their own choosing, while still incorporating elements of the scale in their sequence. For example:

C D E F G F E F E F E F E D C.

Suggestion(s) for support

Some children will manage to play the notes in sequence, but find it difficult to keep an even pulse. Give them plenty of time to practise, and stress that it is simply the *notes* that make the scale, but that it is very useful to be able to play the notes with a steady beat. Those who cannot play the notes in sequence should do the first part of the activity again with your support.

Assessment opportunities

This activity allows you to monitor children's understanding of the concept of scales and their ability to keep a steady beat.

Moving forward

Children can use the knowledge and skills they have gained here for their own composition work, as well as being aware of elements of scales in music they listen to. They can go on to explore the concept of *arpeggios* (musical jumps rather than musical steps) in 'Jumped up Mozart' on page 59.

Composing

For children, composing is often the aspect of music lessons they enjoy most: they can have fun, experiment together and, best of all, have a free range of the instruments. This, of course, coupled with uncertainty about what the children should be doing and how they should react to it, makes the very idea of composing quite terrifying for many teachers. However, the process of composing is the same as in any other creative classroom activity – composing is about making decisions, trying out ideas, evaluating, revising, practising and presenting. (Noise is only a problem if you do not establish clear rules about starting, stopping and use of instruments.) Parallel to this is the process of improvising, where musical decisions are made at the instant of playing. This chapter makes use of both composition and improvisation in a range of different ways, as well as making use of the strong connection between composing and listening.

All the activities can be *adapted* to link with your classroom themes ('Roman sound picture,' for example, could be used to depict Aztecs, Vikings or Victorians), *repeated* to build on the children's developing skills or *extended* over several sessions to give the children the opportunity to evaluate, revise and practise their compositions. If the results sometimes incorporate familiar rhythms or tunes from television, pop music or other aspects of the children's real worlds, do not worry – they will not be the first composers to imitate other people's themes! Suggestions for responding to and extending children's compositions are given on pages 123 and 124.

DICED SOUNDS

To give experience of composing simple rhythms and melodies using tuned and untuned percussion; and of using informal notation.

†† *Whole class then groups of six.*

🕐 *45 minutes.*

♫ *Medium.*

Previous skills/knowledge needed

For this activity children need to be able to keep a steady pulse and have experience in playing simple rhythms and melodies. 'Copy and echo' on page 19 provides this knowledge. 'Mini orchestra' in *Using instruments* in the Key Stage 1 book focuses on playing simple rhythms and tunes.

Key background information

Composing by chance is not a new activity. Mozart concocted a highly complex compositional dice game using small written phrases of music which could follow each other in any order to create a full piece of music. Composition is about choosing sounds and ordering them. Here the child chooses the sounds, but the dice order them.

Vocabulary

Rhythm, ordering, melody, tune.

Preparation

Collect enough dice, one for every group of six children.

Resources needed

Dice, paper, pencils, enough copies of photocopiable sheet 125 for one per group, a selection of tuned and untuned instruments enough for one per child, cassette recorder, microphone capable of recording a class activity, blank cassette.

What to do

Tell the children that they are going to compose a piece of music but the dice is going to be used to decide what it sounds like. Show them photocopiable sheet 125. Explain that every number on the dice needs a tune or a rhythm to go with it, and that they are going to compose these tunes and rhythms. Start with the rhythms. Practise a few rhythms with the children by asking them to keep a steady pulse counting 1 2 3 4, 1 2 3 4 or dum dum dum dum, dum dum dum dum. Ask them to tap louder on each '1'.

When the group is proficient at this, move on to using tuned and untuned percussion instruments. Ask three members of each group to make up a rhythm each that lasts the same amount of time as the 1 2 3 4/dum dum dum dum. The rhythms they make could be a simple 'dum dada dum dum', or 'dada dada dada dada', or one involving silences (or off beats). Tell them to practise playing the *rhythm* they have made on an untuned percussion instrument.

Ask the other three children of each group to make up a simple *tune*. To do this they can use any combination of notes from the range C, D, E, F, G or whatever selection of chime bars you have available. The tunes can have any rhythm the children like but they must fit into the same amount of time as the four-beat rhythms. These very short tunes and rhythms will be composed by the individuals in the group, rather than as a group exercise.

which order they are to play in. If, however, they find this a problem they can write down the order in which the dice number occurred. Instead of written numbers you might like to encourage them to draw the actual dice piece with the number on it.

When they are accustomed to playing the extracts one after another, ask them to make 'rhythm and tune' pairs by putting together odd and even number players. These pairs will play when either of the two children's numbers comes up on the dice. Allow the children to try a few full circles of the dice before asking them to choose their favourite dice composition. Ask them to write the order of this final composition, using signs, symbols, words and/or numbers (see the activities 'Stars in your eyes' on page 106 for grid notation, and 'Graphic notation – instant composition' on page 108 for use of symbols).

Record the compositions and play them back to the children. Ask them to evaluate what they have done. Ask them questions such as: 'What parts do you like best?'; 'Are there any rhythms or tunes on the original dice instruction sheet that you would like to change?'; 'What do you think of the beginning and/or the end?'

Suggestion(s) for extension
As children grow confident with this form of composition ask them to make up rhythms that last for a count of eight rather than four. Instead of having a dice instruction sheet, make a net of a cube for each group and let the children write the different rhythms and tunes directly onto the compositional dice.

Suggestion(s) for support
If children are finding the activity difficult, suggest that they keep the same rhythm for 1, 3 and 5 on the dice recording sheet, while changing the tunes. Give them two chime bars to compose the tunes.

Assessment opportunities
This activity provides opportunities to assess a child's ability to experiment with instruments, make up a simple tune or rhythm, and play from simple notation.

Opportunities for IT
The children could use software such as *Compose World* and give each of the pre-set tunes a number to be played as the dice dictates. Alternatively, they could use the software to make up their own tunes and rhythms to use with the dice.

The children could also use a keyboard and save a selection of tunes and rhythms in the keyboard memory to be used with the dice. If the computer has a MIDI interface the children can compose their own tunes and rhythms on the keyboard and then save them on the computer to be used with the dice.

Give them five to seven minutes to practise individually. Give out the photocopiable sheets and ask each child to write down the rhythm or tune that they have composed. The children who have composed the tune should write it down opposite an even number on the group's sheet, in any way that will help them to remember it. If the child has made up a rhythm, ask her or him to write it down using 'dum' and 'dadas', opposite any odd number on the sheet. Whenever their number comes up on the dice, the child who composed the corresponding tune or rhythm plays it.

The game can now start. The children number themselves in the group (according to their number on their sheet). Number one throws the dice. According to the number that comes up a tune or rhythm will be played. Regardless of who throws the dice, the child who composed that rhythm or tune is the one who plays it. After this first rhythm or tune has been played number two in the group throws the dice. The rhythm or tune that comes up will be played but only after the first extract has been played. Thus the piece starts to accumulate with each new extract being added on to the string of compositions.

Continue round the group until everyone has thrown the dice once. Play through the whole piece, playing the full accumulation of all the extracts one after another, without a break. With only six extracts the children should remember

Display ideas

Use the dice recording sheet and the children's notation sheets to make a big book of music, so that other children can play the tunes they have made. Display the book with the recording of the pieces and leave copies of photocopiable sheet 125 for the listener to write down their view of the pieces of music.

Reference to photocopiable sheet

The photocopiable sheet 125 is used by each group, where they write down the different rhythms and tunes they have made up for each number on the dice.

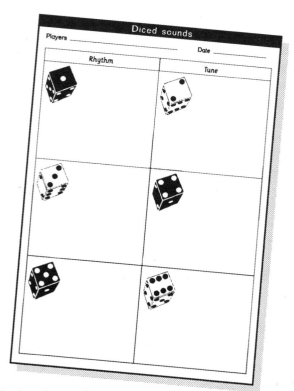

Moving forward

The activity 'Jumped up Mozart' on page 59 develops instrumental skills using grid notation as the form of notation. 'Chartbusters' on page 94 asks the children to make up rhythms, lyrics and a base line, and links well with this activity. The idea of composing by chance was taken up by John Cage, whose work is used as a stimulus for the activity 'Sound cage' on page 68.

ROMAN SOUND PICTURE

To develop the children's ability to choose instruments and compose with them to create a specific effect.

†† *Whole class in groups of four or five.*

🕐 *Three 45-minute sessions. (Session three is optional and concentrates on notating the children's compositions.)*

♬ *Medium.*

Previous skills/knowledge needed

To carry out this activity the children will require knowledge about the Romans and Roman building processes. Musically, they will find it useful to have experience of composing simple rhythms. The activity 'Copy and echo' on page 19 will provide this. The 'Diced sounds' activity in this chapter gives a very structured use of simple melody and rhythm. If you wish children to notate their compositions, 'Stars in your eyes' on page 106 provides a grid notation method, whereas the activity 'Graphic notation – instant composition' on page 108 gives an abstract form of notation.

Key background information

Very little is known about Roman music itself. It is known that they used harps (lyres), flutes and simple trumpets to give signals in the army, and they probably used simple drums. Given that there is little written evidence or source material about either what was played or what it sounded like, it is not worthwhile trying to recreate Roman music as it would have sounded then. In this activity the children are asked to think about what would have been going on when Hadrian's Wall was built and how they could represent this in sound. It is intended that it is more than just sound effects, but a definite musical representation of, in this case, the building of the wall. The activity could be used with a number of topics which you may be doing: Aztecs' way of life, Egyptian pyramid building, Viking raiding parties, or Victorian industrial mills.

Hadrian's Wall was a huge 120-kilometre long, six-metre high wall that was built over a period of two hundred years in Northumberland. It marked the northernmost boundary of the Roman empire. The wall was over three metres wide and was continuously patrolled by soldiers with 'mile' castles offering shelter at regular intervals. It was built by the Roman army and involved hewing the rock, digging the foundations, mixing local lime to make mortar, and constant checks by the army's engineers. The building of Roman roads followed a similar process.

Composing

Vocabulary
Represent.

Preparation
To do this activity satisfactorily you should have covered some work on the Romans and Hadrian's wall (or whatever aspect of life or building process is being represented). A drama session where the children simulate making the wall or working on the construction of a road would be excellent preparation.

Resources needed
A wide selection of tuned and untuned instruments, one copy of photocopiable sheet 126 per group, large sheet of paper and a felt-tipped pen, cassette recorder, blank cassette, pencils.

What to do
Session one
Brainstorm everything the children know about Hadrian's Wall or building a road and write their suggestions on the large sheet of paper. From the brainstorm highlight five or six activities that occurred when the wall was being made. For example, there could be a group of labourers getting stone out of the ground, another group loading it into the cart, the cart travelling to the building place, the stones being levered into place and the mortar being mixed and placed.

Put the children into groups and ask them to choose one of the jobs and think what type of sounds they need to represent the process. Ask them questions such as would it be a slow, difficult job, or a fast, easy job? Would it involve lifting or sliding, a regular rhythm or an irregular chaotic rhythm? Give out the photocopiable sheet and ask the children to fill in the first two sections about the type of job it is – what sound/atmosphere it suggests, and which instruments they want to use to create it.

Remind the children that they are trying to show very specific things in their music, and that you, as the audience, should be able to hear these when they play it. If the job is pulling something very heavy then it should show it in the music. Similarly, if it is soldiers standing about laughing and 'ducking out' of work then the music should show this by the different feeling it creates.

Ask the children to collect the instruments that they require and let them try out their ideas. Give them seven to ten minutes to create their piece. This will sound very loud but do not worry about the noise except of course if it is interrupting colleagues – it is impossible to compose with instruments without making a noise! After five minutes, stop the groups using a pre-agreed stopping sign (see 'Stop and start' on page 14). Remind them of the task and emphasise that the music must show what job it is portraying. Remind them of the advantages of looking at each other and working together as a group. Give them five more minutes before hearing what they have done so far.

This will end the first session. Ask the children to write down their composition in some way on the photocopiable sheet that will help them remember it for next time. Writing down the instruments each child plays is particularly useful.

Session two
Before the children play what they have composed so far, remind them of the task and give out the photocopiable sheets from the previous session. Each group now plays their composition and the rest of the class sees if they can pick out the job that is being portrayed. Respond to each group by commenting on specific things that occur only in their group, such as: 'I like the way you all started together'; 'Tell me about the single triangle beat'; 'How could you make it sound as though the horse and cart were feeling tired or going away again?' Ask the group what they think of their composition and tell them to write down on their sheet one thing they liked about it, one thing that could have been better, and whether they felt it sounded like the activity that was meant to be represented. Then ask the rest of the class what they thought of the piece and make a list of all the suggestions and get the group to whom it applies to write down the suggestions on their photocopiable sheet. Give the group three to four minutes to incorporate the changes in their compositions. Finally, tape a play-through without interruption before ending the session.

It was good when we banged the cymbal for the centurion.

29

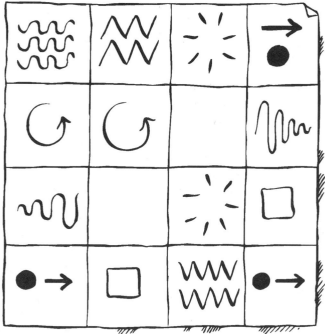

Session three

Play the tape of the recordings from the previous session and ask the children to choose a way to notate their composition. This could take the form of *graphic notation*, notation arranged in a grid form or written description. (See the activity 'Graphic notation – instant composition' on page 108 for an example of this.) What is important is that the composers can understand and follow their notation. As a final challenge, ask each group to hand on their notation to the group next to them, who will then attempt to play the piece from the notation they have been given.

Suggestion(s) for extension

If the children are particularly confident, ask them to represent two or even three activities being seen at the same time. Ask them to compose some sort of movement or walking music between each lot of job music, to represent a visitor to the scene being taken past all the jobs that are going on.

Suggestion(s) for support

If the children are finding the work difficult suggest that they represent a single person doing one thing, for example, a weary soldier slowly walking round looking for his friend, represented by a slow drum beat.

Assessment opportunities

This activity gives the opportunity to assess the children's ability to choose instruments and compose to create a specific sound effect. It also offers the opportunity to observe their ability to perform together and notate their own compositions.

Opportunities for IT

The children could use a multi-media authoring package to make an electronic presentation in which the recorded music is linked to appropriate pictures or text, to create an electronic slide show. The compositions can be recorded using a microphone linked to the computer. The sound files that are created in this way could then be linked to pictures of Hadrian's Wall, or other Roman structures, which could be drawn by the children using an art package, scanned from their own line drawings or photographs, or imported from CD-ROMs.

Display ideas

If the children have notated their piece, use the concept of the wall or road being built as a basis for display. Give each group a 'slab of stone' and ask them to write on this with the first drafts and opinions at the bottom and the most recent comments or revised notation at the top. This forms a useful link to archaeological discovery – the earliest layers are the furthest down and the most recent are at the top.

Maps showing Hadrian's Wall or straight Roman roads could also be displayed.

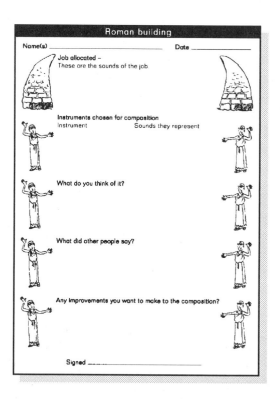

Reference to photocopiable sheet

Photocopiable sheet 126 gives a simple structure for planning the composition. The sheet has space for listing the job and the sounds which represent it, what instruments would be used to play these sounds, and space to write in improvements suggested by the group and other people.

Moving forward

If you wish to reinforce the idea of representation of action or atmosphere, the next activity in this chapter, 'Pavement café', uses composing to create a busy French café.

PAVEMENT CAFÉ

To develop the ability to select and use sounds for composition.

†† *Whole class, then groups of six to eight.*

🕐 *One hour.*

🎵 *Medium.*

Previous skills/knowledge needed

It will help if the children have some experience of careful, focused listening before they do this activity. 'Talking about music' on page 40 incorporates three listening sheets (see pages 129, 130 and 131) which would be particularly useful as a preparation for this activity. An ability to select sounds for a particular effect would also be helpful – 'Roman sound picture' in this chapter could be used for this. For sensitivity to the sound quality of different instruments, 'Controlling timbre' on page 22 provides useful background experience.

Key background information

This activity is an exercise in musical impressionism. Impressionism in music is like impressionism in painting (characterised by the works of French artists such as Monet, Degas and Renoir) where the intention is not to create a finely-detailed finished product, but to suggest scenes or events, to give glimpses and to convey fleeting impressions. A particular Renoir painting is focused on for this activity, together with some alternative suggestions (see 'Preparation').

The composer whose work is most often associated with impressionism in music is Debussy, who used touches of sound in rather the same way as the Impressionist painters used touches of colour and light. (Debussy's 'Preludes' for piano are a good example of this style.) Musical impressionism can also be found in the work of more recent composers, for example Benjamin Britten from England and Charles Ives from the United States. A piece of music by Ives is used as a stimulus for this activity: 'Central Park in the Dark'.

Vocabulary

Impressionism, colour, sound, timbre, Ives, Renoir, Debussy.

Preparation

Listen to the Ives piece (on the cassette that can be purchased to accompany this book) or your own choice of music – see 'Resources needed' – two or three times to familiarise yourself with the sounds and images it uses. Find a copy of Renoir's painting *At the Moulin de la Galette*, painted in 1876, and look at it closely, paying attention to both the overall atmosphere of the scene and the details that make it up. (Alternatives to this painting might be: Renoir's *Le déjeuner des canotiers*, Degas' *Women on the terrace of a café*, and Liebermann's *Oude Vinck*.) Set out the instruments and café items. If you would like the children to evaluate their compositions, make one copy of sheet 151 for each group.

Resources needed

Recording of 'Central Park in the Dark' by Charles Ives, (performed by the Lisbon Gulbenkian Orchestra [Nimbus]), or any other piece of music which uses snatches of sound to create a sound picture, cassette player, blank cassette (optional), a print of Renoir's painting *At the Moulin de la Galette* (or an alternative – see 'Preparation'), enough instruments with a range of timbres (sound qualities) for the whole class, a range of objects to represent the sounds of a pavement café, for example cups, saucers, glasses and cutlery, one copy of photocopiable sheet 151 for each group (if required).

What to do

Play the recording of 'Central Park in the Dark' to the class, without telling them the title. Ask them to consider what images it conjures up while they are listening. After the first time, ask them if they heard sounds which suggested traffic passing by, or a band playing. Tell them that the composer of this piece was painting a picture with music. What sort of place do they think the picture is of? Discuss this with the children, reminding them that the music may conjure up different images in the minds of each of them. (This piece was written at the turn of the century – what was in Ives' mind's eye may be rather different from the images his music conjures up some ninety years later.) Listen again, asking the children to close their eyes and imagine the picture in their heads.

Now that the children have tried creating a picture in their heads from a piece of music, tell them they are going to create a piece of music from a picture. Show them the print of *At the Moulin de la Galette* and discuss the main features: the café itself; the people; the items on the tables; the dancing couples. Tell the children how the picture was created using tiny brush strokes, each meaning nothing in itself but building up an overall impression of colour and light. Ask them what sort of sounds might bring this picture alive. They will probably suggest a combination of café and street sounds, with some dance music in the background. Ask each child in turn to select an instrument or object, or to choose a voice sound to represent one of the themes or events in the picture, and then decide how they will use it. Give them a few minutes to try out possibilities.

Now you can begin to bring the picture to life. Ask the children to select their favourite sound, then rotate your arm slowly and continuously in the air and ask each child to make their sound once when your arm reaches a point of their choice in its circular movement. This creates a pattern of sounds which is repeated with every rotation. Continue for several more rotations, pointing out to the children that the combination of small elements of sound into an overall sound picture is very much like the impressionist painters'

combination of small brush strokes into a whole painting.

Ask them what kind of atmosphere this combination of sounds created. Did it conjure up the feeling of the café? How could it be made more effective? You might try several different combinations and sequences, and discuss your favourites. (If you record each version as it is created, parts of the recordings themselves can be used to create elements of new compositions – see 'Suggestion(s) for extension'.)

Divide the class into groups of six to eight and ask them to create their own sound pictures of the pavement café, using whatever combination of voices, instruments and everyday objects they choose. Suggest that they might like to 'fade in' the music, like a photograph in a developing tray. Remind them that they need to make the listeners feel they are really in the café, so they must think carefully about sounds and atmosphere. Remind them, too, that they should use touches of sound like touches of colour.

Give them about 20 minutes to develop their compositions, then bring the class back together and ask one group to set themselves and their instruments up ready for a performance, while the rest of the class creates a frozen mime of the café, positioning themselves at tables or on the dance floor. As the group plays, ask the other children to gradually 'come to life', making their gestures and movements echo the music. Repeat this with the other groups, until everyone has had a turn at both playing and miming.

If you want to develop these compositions further over future sessions, you might like to use the evaluation sheet on page 151.

Suggestion(s) for extension

Children who show sensitivity and skill in this way of 'painting with sound' can create their own sound pictures from other paintings. The link between touches of colour and touches of sound can be made even clearer by asking these children to create their own impressionist musical 'scores', using different colours to represent different sounds. (See 'Graphic notation – instant composition' on page 108 for an introduction to graphic notation. If you want the children to create graphic scores, they can use sheet 127.

If you have access to a multi-track cassette recorder, you can invite individuals or groups to lay down layers of sound, including recordings from other sources, to create a sophisticated sound picture.

Composing

Suggestion(s) for support

Some children will have difficulty deciding what type of sound to make with their instrument, object or voice. The main point to stress is that it is not the choice of sound that matters so much as the way in which it is used; it is just one of the numerous 'brush strokes' which go to make up the whole sound picture. Ask children who are unsure to listen to the sounds being used by those around them. It may help to ask one group to play their sound picture part-way through the composition process, while the others listen.

Assessment opportunities

This activity enables you to monitor the children's ability to select and use sounds for composition, and to listen carefully both to recorded music and to their own and each others' improvised sounds.

Opportunities for IT

If the children have access to keyboards which have a demonstration or sampling facility, these can be used to generate sounds which can be added to the improvisations. It may also be possible to record different sound effects using a microphone attached to the computer so that a series of sound tracks can be built up and played simultaneously through the computer.

The children could also use an art or drawing package to create their own musical score of the sound pictures and to create their own Impressionist pictures to go with the improvisations. The sound pictures and graphics could be combined using a multi-media authoring package.

Display ideas

A combination of Impressionist paintings and the children's graphic scores of Impressionist music (see 'Suggestion(s) for extension') will make a striking visual demonstration of the link between these two forms of creativity. Poetry could also be added, using words rather than music to represent the images in the painting.

Reference to photocopiable sheets

Photocopiable sheet 151 is an evaluation sheet that invites children to reflect on their own compositions. Photocopiable page 127 provides a frame within which children can write their own graphic scores (see 'Suggestion(s) for extension').

Moving forward

This activity provides a useful preparation for some of the more advanced activities in the *Listening* chapter, for example 'Responding to music' and 'Music review' which form part of 'Talking about music' on page 40. The process of experimenting with sounds in a whole-class improvisation before moving into group compositions is repeated at a more advanced level in 'Composing with voices' in this chapter.

 PERFORMANCE POETRY

To develop rhythmic and vocal skills and the ability to keep in time with others.

†† *Whole class, then groups of four to six.*

🕐 *One hour (or more if you extend the activity over several sessions).*

♩ *Advanced.*

Previous skills/knowledge needed

The children need to have experience in working with rhythms and keeping a beat. 'Copy and echo' and 'Controlling tempo' on pages 19 and 21 would both be useful for this. 'Tudor pastimes' on page 52, and 'Chartbusters' on page 94 would also provide good background experience for this activity, as they have a strong focus on the rhythm of words.

Key background information

Performance poetry can take many forms: it may be a straight forward rhythmic recitation, a combination of voices and other sounds, or even the mixing of electronically sampled words and phrases. This activity could be spread over several sessions to give the children the opportunity to refine and develop their work.

Vocabulary

Rhythm, beat, rap, performance poetry, mood, atmosphere.

Preparation

Listen to the extract from Lemn Sissay's 'Rhythm Rap' on the cassette (or your own choice of music: for example, another contemporary rap piece). Read aloud to yourself several times 'Play No Ball' by Gerard Benson from sheet 128 (or a poem of your choice). Try reading it at different speeds and with different emphasis on each reading. Experiment with different voice tones: sad, authoritative, expectant and so on. Try adding a beat on a drum or your knee, or set up a background rhythm on a keyboard or drum machine if you have one. (Try a rap rhythm in particular – see 'What to do'.) If you want to spread this activity over several sessions, you may also wish to have a copy of the performance evaluation sheet 152 for each group of children.

Resources needed

Recording of extract from Lemn Sissay's 'Rhythm Rap' (from *Rap with Rosen* [Longman Publishing]), or your own choice of music, cassette player, blank cassette (optional), one copy of photocopiable sheet 128 (or your choice of poem – but beware of copyright) for each group and one for yourself, one copy of the performance evaluation sheet 152 for each group if required, two or three percussion instruments for each group, or, if you have electric drum machines or keyboards with percussion effects, one of these for each group.

What to do

Listen to the extract from 'Rhythm Rap'. Talk to the children about the poem and ask them if they know any raps. Play it again, this time setting up a body percussion rhythm with the whole class to go with the rap, using knee-slaps and hand-claps:

knee knee clap *(rest)*
knee knee clap *(rest)*

This gives a basic background rap rhythm, which could be represented like this:

Keep this rhythm going all the way through the recording, making sure you keep in time with the words.

Read 'Play No Ball' to the class twice. The first time, emphasise the meaning of the words by using some of the different voice tones you have experimented with, and the second time, emphasise the rhythm. Talk to the children about the message of the poem and about the different sorts of voices which would be suitable for different parts.

Set up the 'knee knee clap' rhythm again, and once the class is comfortable with this, ask a group of four or five children to repeat the words PLAY – NO – BALL loudly and angrily in time with the rhythm:

knee knee clap __   knee knee clap __
PLAY_____   NO _____
knee knee clap __   knee knee clap __
BALL _____

Composing

They should continue this, keeping up the rhythm and the words without stopping.

Recite the poem against this rhythmic backing, keeping your words in time with the beat. Do this a couple of times, asking the rest of the class to listen and comment on the effect it has.

Explain that they are going to make up their own piece of performance poetry in groups, based on 'Play No Ball'. Each group will need to provide its own rhythm – either a rap rhythm like the one you have been using, or another that they devise themselves, using either percussion instruments or electronic equipment. Against this rhythmic background, the group members will need to decide how they are going to perform the words.

They need to find a way of combining different words and phrases from the poem to create their own special effect, with no more than two people in each group performing the same part.

Here are some examples of what they could do:

▲ One child/pair could recite the poem slowly while another recites it at twice the speed;

▲ One child/pair could repeat a single phrase over and over again as part of the backing rhythm (as with 'Play – no – ball' in the whole-class version) while someone else recites the poem;

▲ Several phrases could be spoken simultaneously by several children/pairs to make a complex rhythm, against which other parts of the poem could be spoken;

▲ Lines from the poem could be sung, chanted, whispered or shouted against each other, with different children taking different lines;

▲ Some members of the group could perform the poem as it is written, while others perform it backwards, culminating in 'What a wall';

▲ The poem could be split into sections, and these performed simultaneously, in time with each other.

Give a copy of the poem (sheet 128) to each group, and give them about 20 minutes to work on the poem. Before they start, remind the children that this is a *composition* activity; they will need to *make decisions* about what to do, *try* their ideas out and *evaluate* the effect before they are ready to perform their work. They will need to *practise* their piece in order to get it right. Suggest to the children that they decide on their background rhythm before starting to rearrange the words.

Ask each group to perform their version of the poem to the rest of the class. Record the results if possible, so that they can hear the effect.

Finally, play the extract from 'Rhythm Rap' again and ask for suggestions as to how this could be rearranged to create a different performance. As a follow-up, they could evaluate their performance using sheet 152. You can then use further sessions to refine and develop each group's work.

Suggestion(s) for extension

Children can compose a performance version of a poem of their own choosing; this might be a poem from an anthology, or one they have written themselves; or they could create their own performance of 'Rhythm Rap'.

Children with a particularly strong sense of rhythm can be invited to create a more complex rhythmic backing for their performance. Encourage them to use skills they may have learned outside school, through listening to pop music or playing drum kits, for example.

Composing

Suggestion(s) for support

As the success of this activity depends upon the children's ability to keep in time with each other, those who find this difficult will need support. Try to pair these children with those who can keep time well, and check that their part of the performance is not too complex. Above all, remind them to *listen* to the rest of their group, and to *hear* how their part fits with the others. Recording the performance will help to make this clear, and continued practice, through this and other activities, will allow them to develop this skill.

Assessment opportunities

Assess the children's ability to use words and rhythms imaginatively, to work co-operatively on a composition and present it as a performance, to hold a part against other performers and to keep in time with each other.

Opportunities for IT

The children could use the rhythm section from a keyboard or suitable music software, such as *Music Box*, to create a rhythmic backing to the performance of the words.

The children could also use a word processor to draft the poem, creating a written version to assist with the performance of the poem. The editing facilities of the word processor will enable them to make frequent changes without having to re-write the poem each time. The teacher could prepare a word-processed file of the poem in advance so that the children could start with this version of the text. The final versions could be printed out and used as a part of a class display.

Display ideas

Poems used for this activity can be displayed along with children's evaluations of their work or comparisons between their own work and that of other composers. If the children have rearranged the poem for performance using a computer, their new versions can be printed and displayed.

Reference to photocopiable sheets

Photocopiable sheet 128 is a copy of 'Play No Ball' by Gerard Benson (1992). This is used as the basis for composition in this activity, where the children use it to create their own piece of performance poetry. Photocopiable sheet 152 invites children to evaluate their own performance.

Moving forward

The use of voices leads to the freer exploration of voice sounds in the next activity, 'Composing with voices'. This activity also links well with 'Streetwise' on page 101, which has a strong focus on the rhythm of words.

Composing

 ## COMPOSING WITH VOICES

To develop the use of voices as musical instruments and their creative use in composition.

†† *Whole class, then groups of six to eight.*

🕐 *One hour (or 2 x 30-minute sessions).*

♫ *Advanced.*

Previous skills/knowledge needed

The children need to have experience of controlling the pitch of their voices and in listening to each other sensitively: 'Controlling pitch' and 'Controlling timbre' on pages 15 and 22 provide this. The activity also leads on from 'Performance poetry', as it invites the children to make a further exploration of the use of their voices as musical tools. However, neither you nor the children have to be experienced singers to carry out this activity; it is about exploring and using voice sounds, not about singing tunes.

Key background information

This activity concentrates on the use of the voice as a musical instrument, starting with an example from 16th Century *polyphony*, where it is the rise and fall of voices against each other which produces its particularly haunting effect. An extract from a *Mass for Five Voices* by William Byrd (on the cassette) is used as a stimulus, but any piece of sacred vocal music from this period could be used, or contemporary music (for example, New Age music or relaxation tapes) which makes atmospheric use of voice sounds.

Vocabulary

Voices, atmosphere, pitch, harmony, polyphony, improvisation, composition.

Preparation

Listen to the 'Kyrie' from the *Mass for Five Voices* (or your own choice of music). Notice the way in which the voices rise and fall in relation to each other, creating unusual harmonies. If you would like the children to evaluate their compositions or performances, make a copy of sheet 151 or sheets 154 and 155 for each child.

Resources needed

Recording of the 'Kyrie' from William Byrd's *Mass for Five Voices* (Naxos), or your own choice of music, cassette player, blank cassette (optional), copies of photocopiable sheets 151, 154 and 155 for each child (optional).

What to do

Stand the whole class in a circle in a large space. Without any introduction, play Byrd's 'Kyrie' to the class, then, as soon as it has finished, start one section of the circle (about a quarter) humming a low, sustained note. Keep this note going, and invite the next section of the circle to join in humming a slightly higher note. Add two more notes with the remaining two sections, so that the whole circle is humming.

Now use hand signals so the humming becomes louder and quieter. It is suggested that you move your hands apart for louder and together for quieter; you will be moving your hands up and down to indicate pitch next.

When the class is responding well, reduce the volume of the humming, and while they are still humming quietly, tell the children that you want them to change the pitch of their note, following your hand signals. At first, move both hands up or down at the same time, then indicate that half the class should follow one hand and the other half should follow the other, and make your hands go in opposite directions, so that the pitch of one half of the circle rises while that of the other half falls. (You can use child conductors here if you wish: see 'Suggestion(s) for extension'.) Finally, without stopping, ask all the children following one hand to sing their notes to 'Ah' while the others continue to hum. Listen to the sounds they are making, and when they reach a particularly pleasing combination, hold the notes then use a hand signal to stop the music.

Sit with the children and discuss the sounds they heard on the recording and the sounds they have been making themselves. (You may wish to use the term 'polyphony' to describe the music on the recording.) What sort of atmosphere did these sounds create? What was the effect when half the circle changed from humming to singing? Explain that they have been using their voices as instruments, and that they are going to create their own compositions for voices. If you are running this activity over two sessions, finish the first one here.

Explain to the class that the piece of music they have been making with their voices was an *improvisation*: the exact combinations of sounds were not planned beforehand, but grew out of the decisions of the singers and the conductor.

Tell them that they are now going to use improvisation, working in groups, to explore voice sounds from which they will create a *composition*. They can restrict themselves to changes in pitch and volume as in the whole-class improvisation if they wish, or they can experiment with different styles and effects, as long as they only use voices. Remind them that, as they are working in quite large groups, they can incorporate several different parts into their compositions if they wish, or they can use the strength of the combined voices to create a body of sound in unison. They may like to have sounds coming from different places, as they did in the whole-class improvisation. The important thing is to *listen* to the sounds they are making at all times, in order to decide whether they wish to use them or not.

Give the groups about 20 minutes to create their compositions, reminding them that this process will involve selecting, evaluating, revising and practising. Ask each group

to perform their composition to the rest of the class. Record the performances if you can, so the children can evaluate them later. For the performances, stand the children in their groups in a circle. When all the groups have performed, ask them to perform their compositions again, but to stop and start in response to your signals. Conduct the groups in and out of this composite performance, listening carefully to the combinations of sounds and asking the children to do the same. This will create a peculiar effect: some of it will sound pleasant and some unpleasant. You can experiment with combinations of different groups and, as with the improvisation at the beginning of the activity, stop when you feel you have reached a particularly pleasing or interesting combination of sounds.

Discuss the different groups' compositions and the effect of combining them into a single piece. Conclude the activity by playing the 'Kyrie' again so that the children can compare Byrd's work with their own. You may like them to follow up this activity by using the composition and performance evaluation sheets on pages 151, 154 and 155.

Suggestion(s) for extension
You may wish to use children who are responding to this activity sensitively as conductors during the whole-class improvisations. This will give them the valuable experience of controlling a whole 'orchestra' of voices.

Children who have responded well to group work can experiment with creating different effects by use of a wider range of voice sounds. For example, they might contrast long and short sounds, or sharp and gliding sounds, or they may wish to add a rhythmic or repetitive element. These children could notate their compositions using graphic notation (see page 108 in the *Notation* chapter).

Suggestion(s) for support
Some children will feel very self-conscious about using their voices. They will feel safest if they do not feel too exposed, so make sure they are among other children with more confidence. Some children will have difficulty controlling the pitch and volume of their voices. You may find it useful to return to some of the *Basic skills* activities to reinforce this: for example, 'Controlling pitch' and 'Controlling volume' on pages 15 and 17.

Assessment opportunities
Observe the children's control of the pitch, volume and timbre (sound quality) of their voices and their ability to use them creatively for composition. You will also be able to note their ability to apply the compositional skills they have learned through other activities.

Reference to photocopiable sheets
Photocopiable sheet 151 asks the children to evaluate their compositions, while sheets 154 and 155 are performance evaluation sheets.

Moving forward
Try repeating the improvisations in a large space such as the school hall, spreading the children out so that their voices come from different places. (This technique was used very effectively by composers of the sixteenth and seventeenth centuries.) Alternatively, you could give the activity a more twentieth-century contemporary flavour by incorporating more unusual voice sounds. The focus on listening in this activity leads well into activities in the *Listening* chapter. The link with 'Listening collage' on page 48 is particularly strong, as it demands a similar awareness of the layers of sound which go to make up a composition.

Listening

All the activities in this book are about listening, for the simple reason that music is as much about listening as playing or composing. However, this chapter introduces and develops specific skills and language for listening, as well as focusing on emotional responses. The first activity ('Talking about music') outlines a range of language-based approaches to listening, while the rest of the chapter explores other responses, from comparison and analysis to drawing and collage. None of the activities require specialised musical vocabulary, although a few simple musical terms are introduced by the vocabulary sheets 129, 130 and 131 in 'Talking about music'. You do not need to have any specialist knowledge to do the activities – it is perfectly possible for you to listen and explore along with the children. The aim of the chapter is to get the children listening and responding to the music, not to make them experts. They can reflect on their listening skills by using sheets 156 and 157 (see *Assessment* chapter).

Some of the activities relate to specific pieces of music (available on the cassette that can be purchased to accompany this book), although they can be easily adapted to other pieces and, in most cases, we leave the choice of music up to you. It is a good idea to work with very short extracts (one to two minutes is often enough) for concentrated listening, though you may want to listen to the whole piece as well, to set the extract in context. There are no rules – choose what you like, know or find interesting, and enjoy it.

TALKING ABOUT MUSIC

To develop musical vocabulary, musical awareness and the ability to listen purposefully.

†† *Individuals/groups/whole class.*

⏱ *20-60 minutes.*

♪ *Easy/medium/advanced depending on how the sheets are used.*

Key background information

One of the most important things children need to learn about listening and responding to music is that it is an active, not a passive, activity. The listener's response may be based in language, in a visual medium (as in some of the other activities in this chapter) or purely in the listener's mind – but to be 'real' listening, rather than just hearing, there must be a *response* of some sort. The photocopiable sheets used here offer a range of ways of approaching listening in an active way – searching for descriptive words, expressing opinions and preferences, writing reviews, analysing composers' techniques, interpreting and comparing. Suggestions are provided for *timbre* and *texture* vocabulary (in addition to general vocabulary) as these tend to be the areas that cause teachers the most anxiety. The sheets can be used at any level of difficulty, either as they are or by selecting elements from them. They are referred to in other activities throughout the book and they can also stand alone as activities in themselves.

Vocabulary

Varied, depending on sheets used.

Preparation

Select the photocopiable sheet or sheets you want and decide whether they are to be used as a stimulus for discussion or as worksheets for children to use individually, in pairs or in groups.

Resources needed

Photocopiable sheets 129 to 136 of your choice.

What to do

As explained above, you can use the photocopiable sheets in a variety of ways and adapt them to suit your own needs.

Vocabulary – general, timbre [type of sound], texture (combinations of sound)

Photocopiable sheets 129, 130 and 131 suggest a range of words that could be used to describe music. They include some specialist musical terms, such as 'orchestral', 'duet', and 'timbre', but most of the words come from everyday language. Children will develop their understanding (and their vocabulary) through discussing how words like *thunderous*, *crunchy* or *warm* can be used to describe a piece of music.

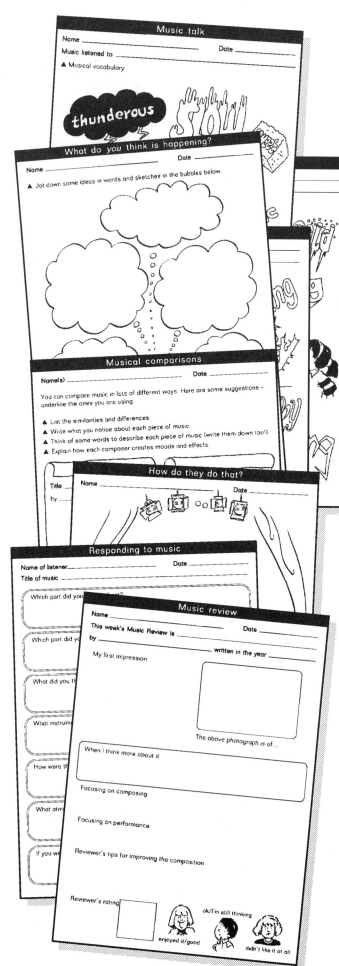

There are no right answers here; you are free to choose your own interpretations, and you may find a lot of disagreement within the class.

What do you think is happening?

Photocopiable sheet 132 invites children to visualise the image a piece of music suggests to them, then describe it and draw it. Music which describes a scene or event would be the most suitable for this, such as 'Fingal's Cave' – this is sometimes called programme music. A tone poem is a type of programme music, often based on a literary or atmospheric scene, for example, Debussy's *La Mer*. This sheet is used for the activity 'Telling tales: music for ballet' on page 62.

Musical comparisons

Photocopiable sheet 133 invites children to compare two pieces of music; these might be examples of live or recorded music, their own compositions, or a combination of any of these. Children can draw attention to the similarities and differences between the two chosen pieces by joining them with lines or arrows, or by using colour coding, or writing linking words onto the sheet. This sheet is used for a number of activities including 'Composing with voices' on page 37 and 'Jumped up Mozart' on page 59.

How do they do that?

Photocopiable sheet 134 is used by the children to analyse the techniques a composer uses to create an atmosphere or effect. You can either focus on a single aspect of the music (for example, the composer's use of dynamics or timbre) or look at it in a more general way, highlighting a variety of techniques. For example, you might combine on a single sheet comments like 'He makes a sudden loud crash – to make us frightened of the enchanter' and 'There is an uneven rhythm – this creates a feeling of restlessness'. (The sheet could be used in this way, for example, as an extension to 'Telling tales: music for ballet' on page 62.) The sheet has an oval shape in the centre – the children can describe the technique ('he makes a sudden loud crash') *inside* the oval and link it to a description of the effect it creates ('to make us frightened of the enchanter') *outside* the oval.

Responding to music

Photocopiable sheet 135 offers children a framework for describing and reflecting on music they have heard. It invites responses at a fairly simple level, such as descriptions and immediate impressions (for example, 'Which part did you like best?')

Music review

Photocopiable sheet 136 invites a more complex response to music, starting with first impressions, then asking children to think again, going on to focus on both the composing and performing aspects of the piece.

Suggestion(s) for extension

Ask children who are working successfully with the ideas above, to devise their own listening sheets or activities for the rest of the class.

Suggestion(s) for support

Some children may respond very sensitively to music, but find it hard to put their thoughts into words, particularly in a written form. It is worth remembering that listening, at least in this context, is a *music* activity, not a *language* activity – you may be able to support these children best by offering the language yourself.

Assessment opportunities

The approaches to listening described here will give you numerous opportunities to monitor children's developing ability to listen carefully and purposefully. It will also show their ability to use an appropriate vocabulary to describe music. You will gain an impression of each child's sensitivity and perception in responding to music.

Display ideas

Any of the photocopiable sheets described here can be displayed alongside relevant facts relating to the compositions they describe. If you place recordings of the music with the display, other people can listen and compare their own opinions with those the children have expressed.

Reference to photocopiable sheets

See 'What to do' for a description of the sheets in this activity and how they are used elsewhere.

Moving forward

The photocopiable sheets used in these activities can be used very successfully with almost any activity in this book. It is important to remember that the skills developed here relate as much to children listening to their *own* compositions as to those of other composers. For this reason, it is a particularly good idea to use them in conjunction with the activities in the *Composing* chapter.

MUSICAL PRINTOUT

To develop concentrated listening and the ability to express opinions about a piece of music.

♫♫ *Whole class or any size of group.*

🕐 *20 minutes.*

♫ *Easy.*

Previous skills/knowledge needed

The children will need previous experience in listening to music of any type.

Key background information

All music has changes in pitch. In some music it will be an easily audible, exaggerated change in pitch. In others it will be more subtle and harder to hear. The overwhelming impression of the up and down might come from the melody or the accompaniment. For this activity it does not matter. Children find fun in the process of conveying what their ears are hearing to their hand and a pen, which means that they listen to the music with greater interest.

Preparation

Decide on the music you want to work with. It can be from any style, century or area of the world – all music lends itself to this activity. However, it is advised that you choose some which has easily audible changes at first ('Take Five' by Dave Brubeck is available on the cassette). Do not feel that you can only listen to one type of music. The children will always benefit from a wide range of listening. The wider choice you can give them, the better it will be for their music education. If you are not feeling confident try the activity out yourself beforehand. (See the illustration below for an idea of what the finished printout might look like.)

Resources needed

Music you wish to use, cassette (with a counter if possible but it is not essential), plain paper, pencils.

What to do

Tell the children that they are going to listen to a short extract of music and that you want them to draw the pattern the music makes by using a single line. Suggest the example of the printout of a heartbeat so that they have an idea of what is required. Give out the pencils and paper, but ask the children just to listen the first time round. Play the music for two minutes. Either use the tape counter or time how long the extract is. When the extract is finished, wind the tape back and without pause, play it again. This time ask the children to draw the line (up and down) as they listen to the music. The children will almost certainly say that they find this difficult and appear discouraged. Reassure them by explaining that you are going to play it four more times and you do not expect anyone to get all of the ups and downs the first time round (or indeed, ever).

Play the extract four times or more, if the children are enjoying it. At first the drawing will be difficult but after a few hearings you will see them beginning to know where they are on the printout at particular moments in the music. You may see the children drawing high peaks of sound when the music is loud; this is an interesting point to note as it shows

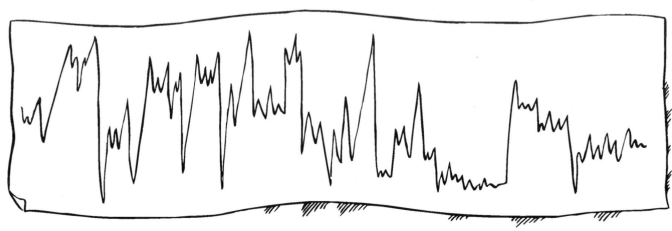

that there is a confusion between high and loud or pitch and volume. You might wish to mention this as a teaching point or merely register it for future planning.

Play the music again and ask the children to pair up and one of each pair show their partner how their printout fits the music. As the music plays they can use the blunt end of their pencils to point at the graph. The children will not always know where particular places in the music are but you will see them suddenly jumping a small section to point to a particular feature of their graph that they recognise. Remember it is not a question of right or wrong, merely a way of getting the children to listen with acute attention to help them to familiarise themselves with what they hear.

Once the children are confident with their graphs ask them to point to the place that shows the part they liked best. Can they say what instruments were playing and write them on the graph? What were the loudest, quietest, highest and lowest parts? Is their graph pointed, jagged, smooth and/or flowing? Does the graph show a pattern? If so, is this reflected in the music?

Suggestion(s) for extension

If the children are finding this activity easy, ask them if they can hear the highest/lowest tunes or rhythms of the piece and draw them on their graph with a different-coloured pencil, so that there are two (or three) graph lines. Alternatively, ask them to try and pick out what the brass, strings or drums do and draw specific lines for these instruments. Tell them to think up a question they would want to ask another child about their graph, such as: Where is your favourite bit? What is the loudest/quietest part of the music? Is there a repeated pattern in the music? How have you shown this?

Suggestion(s) for support

There is no 'right' answer in this activity and some children may find this hard to grasp. Support them by sitting next to them and drawing your own graph. Ask them to show you their favourite part of the music.

Assessment opportunities

Watching the children while they are drawing the graph and listening to the music, provides an excellent opportunity to observe their listening concentration and their ability to distinguish between high and low notes (pitch awareness).

Opportunities for IT

The children could use a microphone attached to the computer to create a graph of the wave form of the sounds which shows the changes in pitch as the music is played. The children could compare these with the music lines they drew as they listened. Other sound sensors could be linked to the computer which will also show changes in the volume while the music is played. These sensors give children an introduction to the idea of computer monitoring or sensing.

The children could re-create their lines using an art or drawing package. They could show different instruments in different colours or add annotations to the lines using the text facilities of the software.

A more sophisticated approach would be for the children to design a numerical representation of the sound lines so that they could be recorded on a database or spreadsheet, graphs drawn and different musical patterns compared. High points could be given a plus score and low points a negative score, with a five-point scale showing variation. The same could be done for pitch as well as volume.

Display ideas

The finished printouts make a very eye-catching display, especially if the children's views on the music are written alongside. Labelling different parts of the graph with points such as 'this is where the sitar comes in' provides information and interest.

Moving forward

If you wish to develop the children's vocabulary to talk about music they have heard, photocopiable sheets 129, 130 and 131 could be used. If you wish to develop their ability to have opinions about what they have listened to, 'Responding to music' and 'Music review' on sheets 135 and 136 would follow on well from this activity and enable you to do this.

JOURNEY LINE

To develop awareness of mood within music and introduce the concept of representing this in an abstract form.

✝✝ *Whole class or any size of group.*

🕐 *30 minutes (though more time may be required to finish the art work).*

♫ *Medium.*

Key background information

All music, whatever its style or cultural background, has changes in atmosphere, speed, loudness and mood. Music can conjure up a set of strong images or colours in a listener's mind, which change as the music progresses. Thinking and talking about music should always include reference to the atmosphere and mood of the piece and we should be aiming to develop the children's own creative response. Abstract symbols and signs can be used to represent not only the actual sound heard, but also the type of atmosphere and feeling present. Graphic notation is the term used to describe the use of signs and symbols in this way. The finished 'journey line' might look like the illustration below.

Preparation

Decide on the music you want to work with. 'Take Five' is given on the cassette (that can be purchased to accompany this book) as a possible piece to use. The first two minutes of the first movement of Beethoven's *Ninth Symphony* also works well with this activity. Choose music that either fits *naturally* with a classroom theme or is a completely disconnected piece which you like. Do not make tenuous connections for the sake of a topic.

Resources needed

Cassette player, recording of 'Take Five' performed by Dave Brubeck, written by Paul Desmond (Sony), or your own choice of music, art materials and A4 paper for each child, access to a white board or a large sheet of paper, thick marker pen.

What to do

Explain to the children that you are going to play them a short piece of music which they are then going to draw on paper, using patterns to show what they think the music is like. Tell them that you will ask them to close their eyes and think about colours, shapes, patterns and/or events that the music makes them think of. Emphasise that for this

exercise you are not interested in a story, but in patterns and colours. It is often helpful to show the children what you mean by putting symbols and patterns on a line. Draw a long line on the white board or paper and add spiral, curly or jagged patterns to it. Beware of them thinking that they have to copy your example! Give out a sheet of paper to each child and ask them to draw a single line across the page like this:

Play the music for about two minutes. Time the extract so that the children will be hearing the same part of the music each time. After the first playing the children will probably still lack confidence and believe that the activity is too hard. Ignore the cries of 'I can't do it' and remind the children of what you want them to do. Reassure them that everyone finds it difficult to start off with, but that they all can do it eventually. Play the music again. To help them pick out themes, you could ask them specific questions. For instance:
▲ Does the music feel the same all the way through?
▲ How does it start: loud, soft, clashing, smoothly, jagged?
▲ What sort of patterns do you want to use to show this?

Ask the children to pick out the colours they want to use for the beginning of the piece. Ask them to experiment with the patterns, shapes and symbols that the music conjures up for them, and then to draw the start of the piece. Play the extract of the piece four or five times more leaving three or four minutes between each playing for the children to draw out their ideas and complete the rest of the extract.

Play the music one more time and ask the children to close their eyes and see if there are any final changes they want to make. Allow them to finish the art work in their own time. As their work is completed ask them about the colours and patterns they have used. Try to use as open-ended questions as possible, for instance:
▲ It's interesting the way you've used yellow, can you tell me about it?

▲ Can you tell me about your triangular pattern?
▲ The red spiral is very striking, can you explain why you put it there?

Suggestion(s) for extension
If children find the activity easy, extend the detail that you are asking them to put on the journey line. Ask them to think how they could represent the change from one mood to another, for example mixing or fading in colour. Perhaps they could write words describing the music on the journey line. Suggest that they introduce another medium, such as ink, pastel or charcoal, and ask them which parts of the music they would want to use it for.

Suggestion(s) for support
Some children may find the concept of representing music in symbols or patterns very hard. Ask them to listen to one sound and talk about the type of shape they could use for it. Does the music make them think of a happy or a sad thing? Tell them to decide which colours they want to use for the happy or sad parts.

Assessment opportunities
This activity provides an excellent opportunity to assess children's understanding of the use of patterns and symbols to represent music, and their ability to transfer sound into abstract form. In addition their ability to talk about music can be assessed.

Opportunities for IT
The children could use an art package to draw their lines. They could experiment with drawing tools, such as brushes, pencils or sprays, to get the effects they want. They could change the line thickness or colour. Areas around the line could be worked on as well to give background effects for mood or atmosphere. While they are working on this, the children could listen to a CD played through the computer's CD-ROM drive with headphones so that they do not disturb other children around them.

Display ideas
The finished journey lines would make a marvellous display, especially if the children make written explanations of their art work to be placed alongside.

Moving forward
This activity can be used again and again with different pieces of music. If you want to continue with the same piece of music, the 'Responding to music' sheet 135 in 'Talking about music' in this chapter uses another approach. 'Listening collage', also in this chapter, develops the children's skill in responding to music, using a different medium.

THE STYLE GAME

To develop children's ability to distinguish between different musical styles.

†† *Whole class.*

🕐 *50 minutes.*

♫ *Medium.*

Previous skills/knowledge needed

This activity can be carried out successfully with very little previous experience. However, using the music vocabulary sheets 129, 130 and 131 would be a good preparation, as they would provide the children with words to describe what they hear.

Key background information

The purpose of this activity is to help children to hear the *differences* between styles of music, rather than giving them detailed knowledge of composers or styles (although this may develop incidentally, and can be seen as an extra bonus). It does not require the teacher to have specialist knowledge of specific composers or specific styles, or to have recordings of particular pieces of music. It can be easily adapted to whatever resources you have to hand, and you can take pleasure in listening and matching with the children.

Anyone who has heard music probably has some ability to discriminate between musical styles. For example, a child of seven could probably distinguish pop from church music, or jazz from classical music, although they might not know what names to apply to them. Children who have seen Walt Disney's *Aladdin* will have some idea of what might characterise Arabic music, while those who have seen *Fantasia* may find that they recognise the music of Bach, Beethoven or Tchaikovsky when they hear it elsewhere. This activity builds on this sort of incidental knowledge, and helps children to clarify what it is that distinguishes one musical style from another.

Vocabulary

Classical, jazz, folk, pop (depending on the styles you use), together with descriptive vocabulary relating to styles.

Preparation

Collect some recordings of two different styles of music, for example, pop and classical, or jazz and folk. You will need four or five examples of each. Bear in mind that you will not be listening to more than one minute of music at a time for most of this session, so choose a suitable short section from each (the middle of a piece is sometimes more useful than the beginning).

Resources needed

Cassette player, recordings of music of two different styles (you could select a range of pieces from the cassette), white board/easel and paper, pens (it helps to have two colours – one for each style of music).

What to do

Sit the children where they can see you and the white board/easel. Have your music-playing equipment nearby, so you do not have to move every time you want to listen to a piece.

Introduce the activity as a musical matching game. Tell the children you are going to play two different pieces of music (play them a sample of each of the two different styles). Do not discuss the characteristics of the music at this stage, other than to reinforce the fact that there are differences between them. After listening, tell them the names of each piece, and write them in different colours on the board. Divide the board space in half so that the pieces you listen to can be listed in two columns. Now play a succession of other pieces, asking each time, 'Is this one more like... (the first

piece you listened to) or more like... (the second piece)?' List the names of the pieces on the board as you go, using the appropriate colour. Leave enough spaces between the names to add comments later.

Once the children are comfortable with listening and decision-making, you can start asking them why they made their choices. You might get answers like: 'Because it uses the sort of instruments you get in an orchestra', 'It's got a strong drum beat' or 'She's singing in a posh voice'. The children may need prompting at first. Here are some questions you could ask:

▲ Where do you think you might hear this sort of music?
▲ Do you know any music that sounds a bit like this?
▲ What sort of instruments can you hear?
▲ What sort of voices are they using?
▲ Do you think this music is old-fashioned or modern?
▲ Do you think this might be music for dancing to?
▲ What sort of dancing might it be for?

Accept all the children's answers, and write them on the board under the music titles. Listen to the first two pieces again and ask what makes them different from each other. List these answers too. Ask the children if they know what sorts of music they have been listening to. Name the two styles (for example, pop and classical) and label each column on the board with the appropriate name. Look at the descriptions written on the board about each of the two types of music, and discuss them with the children. Summarise what you have found out about the styles from this matching game, for example:

> *The classical music we have been listening to uses orchestral instruments. We have heard music like this on television and in films. It sometimes makes us think of the countryside or old-fashioned scenes. You could waltz or ballet dance to this music, but we don't think you would hear it at a disco.*
>
> *We have been listening to some pop music. We dance to this sort of music at discos and hear it on the radio and pop videos. This music sounds modern. Listening to this music makes us want to move, and it sometimes makes us happy or sad because it is often about people loving each other, or not loving each other any more.*

Finish the session by asking them to choose their favourite piece of music, and play it again or a longer excerpt from it (or the whole piece if it only lasts a few minutes, if available). Before you play it, ask them to remind you of the characteristic features you might expect to hear.

Suggestion(s) for extension

Children who find this sort of style-matching easy might compare three or even four different styles. Alternatively, they could compare styles within *one* piece of music. For example, many pop songs have accompaniments which use orchestral instruments more often associated with classical music (for example, 'All you need is love' by the Beatles). Similarly, a lot of classical music uses folk tunes, usually to characterise a country scene or to indicate national pride. Examples of this are Beethoven's *Pastoral Symphony* or *Ma Vlast* (My Country) by the Czechoslovakian composer Smetana. The children could also make a list of the words that they think characterise a certain style.

Suggestion(s) for support

Some children may find it very difficult to distinguish between different pieces of music, or to have a clear idea of what they are looking for. It will help to focus on specific questions about the music with these children (see the suggestions in 'What to do'), and perhaps to sit with them as they are listening and talk about what they can hear. As the activity progresses, the comments offered by the rest of the class will help these children to build up an idea of the characteristics of each style.

Assessment opportunities

This activity allows you to observe the children's awareness of musical style and their ability to listen to music analytically. You will also be able to gauge their previous knowledge of different types of music.

Opportunities for IT

The children could extend this work using multi-media authoring software to create a music-style quiz where excerpts of the music style are recorded using a microphone attached to the computer or sampled from a CD-ROM. Each question in the quiz could have its own screen with an icon (picture) to get the sound sample to play. The possible answers would be displayed in text from which children must select the correct one. If they select the wrong one, an excerpt of this incorrect style could be provided so the user can compare it with the correct one.

Screens might look like this:

Display ideas

A display on 'What we know about... (pop music/classical music)' could be set up. Further details could be added as the children learn more about, for example, the names of pieces or composers, or instruments that are typical of each style. Reviews of pieces of music the children have listened to (perhaps using the photocopiable sheets 135 and 136) could be incorporated. Photographs of musicians performing (orchestras, pop groups, folk bands, jazz bands) would give viewers of the display the opportunity to link a musical style with visual images.

Moving forward

This activity is good preparation for more detailed analytical listening, such as that found in 'Pattern tracking' on page 96. The children's discussions of stylistic features will prepare them well for more advanced tasks within the activity 'Talking about music' in this chapter.

LISTENING COLLAGE

To develop children's awareness of structure and texture in music.

†† *Individuals/groups/whole class.*

🕐 *55 minutes for initial music session; art work could continue over many sessions, depending on individuals.*

♫ *Advanced.*

Previous skills/knowledge needed

Children need to be able to listen to music in a range of ways and react with different responses. The 'Journey line' activity helps to develop confidence in representing music in an abstract form, while 'Musical printout' develops concentration in listening to music (both these activities are in this chapter). Any work done with the photocopiable sheets 129 to 136 will mean that the children are already used to thinking and talking about music and will, therefore, find the activity easier to do. If you wish to use words on the collage (see 'Suggestion(s) for extension'), previous work on the music vocabulary sheets 130 and 131 describing timbre and texture will prove useful. The activity 'Pattern tracking' on page 96 will give the children experience of hearing different strands in music, and they can represent these using art materials in this activity. 'Composing with voices' on page 37 will reinforce understanding of lines of sound interwoven with each other.

Key background information

Pachelbel was born in Germany in 1653. His most famous piece is his *Canon*. A 'canon' is a piece of music where the instruments play the same thing, but come in at different times. In Pachelbel's piece there is a bass line which is repeated continuously throughout. A bass line like this is known as a *ground bass* (also known as a 'ground'). It is fairly common in music of this period. Ground bass can often be found in contemporary pop music where the keyboards or bass guitar repeat the same bass line throughout the piece.

Vocabulary

Interweaving, chunky, blocks of sound, threads of sound, high, low, dense, airy, melody, harmony, bass line.

Preparation

Listen to the extract from Pachelbel's *Canon* (available on the cassette) so that you are familiar with the main tune in the top line and the main repeated tune in the bass. It might be helpful to re-record the first two bars of the extract four times so that you do not have to keep winding the tape back.

Collect together a range of art mediums, including different textures and colours of materials and paper, pastels, pencils, crayons. You might wish to make a copy of the music vocabulary sheet 131 for the children to use if they have not concentrated on texture in music before.

Resources needed

Recording (approximately the first three minutes) of Pachelbel's *Canon and Gigue in D Major* (from *Baroque Festival* [Naxos] or your own version), cassette recorder, pastels, different kinds of paper and materials for collage work, A3 paper, adhesive, scissors. Optional: photocopiable sheet 131.

What to do

Tell the class that they are going to listen to some music which they will then be representing in collage form. Have a practice first. Play them the first two bars of the *Canon* repeated four times so that the children become familiar with it. Brainstorm words they think describe it. Ask them to suggest words that describe the texture of it, for example, smooth, chunky, rough, in addition to words such as interweaving, spiky, oily. (Give out photocopiable sheet 131 if necessary.) Now ask them to choose the materials that they would like to use for this piece of the music, cut or tear the materials into shapes and stick them onto the A3 paper in a combination that they think best represents the music. Some of the children will need encouragement and support in representing a sound with materials. Emphasise that there is no right or wrong way and that it is up to them to decide what they are going to use from listening to the music.

Once the trial run is done, play them the first minute of the music. Time it so that you know how far in the piece you have gone. Stop the music and discuss what you have heard. Ask them questions such as:

▲ How many instruments were playing at the beginning of the extract? Did the same number of instruments continue to play?

▲ What sort of sounds were they making?

▲ Were they higher or lower than the first part of the piece?

▲ What words would they use to describe this tune?

▲ What materials and shapes would they use to represent it and where would they place it in relation to the first part?

At this point the children will have to decide how they are going to lay out their collage and whether they are going to try and fit the whole piece on one sheet of paper. A spiral line of the music could be the basis for the collage part; they could represent the feel of the piece without trying to show every single part of it. (See illustration below.)

Offer suggestions and leave the children to make up their own minds. Remind them again that there are no right or wrong answers. Some children will want to start a new piece of paper, while others will be happy to use their practice piece. Those who wish to use a fresh sheet can always tear off their collage of the first few bars from their first sheet and stick it onto the new one. Play the piece again from the beginning for a minute and let the children choose materials for their collage and start to build up their work. Play the piece two or three more times using the full extract (which is only a part of the whole piece) and let the children continue their collage. You might want to make comments such as 'I love that reddy-orange patch, tell me about it', 'Which is your favourite part of the collage?' or 'How have you represented the repeated bass line?'

Ask the children to show and explain their collage to a friend. Tell them to talk about the parts where they feel they have really captured (represented) the music, and the parts where this has not happened. The collages may take more than one session but the time spent will be well worth it.

Suggestion(s) for extension

If some children find this activity easy, develop their project by asking them to include words describing the music, at suitable places in the collage. They could do this using their own handwriting or letters cut from a newspaper.

Suggestion(s) for support

If the children are finding the activity hard, ask them to represent only one part of the music (maybe their favourite part), or only one instrument.

Assessment opportunities

This activity provides opportunities to assess children's awareness of the concept of texture in music, their developing vocabulary and ability to talk about music, and their abstract responses to it.

Opportunities for IT

The children could use an art package to create their own collage. They could experiment with different colour shades or pattern mixes. Different effects could be created using patterns, brushes of different thicknesses, rollers or spray cans. The children may also need to know how to create simple shapes and pictures, sometimes called stamps, which they can place, copy and move around within the picture to give ideas of repeating patterns of shapes and sounds. They could work in different shades or patterns of the same colour, depending on the mood the music created for them.

Display ideas

The collages, with an explanation by the children of the project, will make an excellent display. If you have done the 'Journey line' activity display, it could be placed alongside for comparison.

Reference to photocopiable sheet

Photocopiable sheet 131 is a list of music vocabulary describing texture. This would be useful to support the children's ability to talk about the texture of the music.

Moving forward

You may feel that you want to complement the children's music listening experience by using the 'Talking about music' activity sheets. Alternatively, you could repeat the activity using a completely different piece of music, such as rock 'n' roll, with a repeating bass line.

Classical Music

You do not have to be an enthusiast or an expert to explore classical music in the classroom. The aim of this chapter is to show ways of demystifying classical music and making it accessible both to the teacher and the children. The chapter travels through the key periods of Western classical music: from Tudor music (sixteenth century), through the Baroque period (seventeenth century, associated with composers such as Bach, Handel and Vivaldi), to the confusingly-named Classical period (eighteenth century, represented most famously by Mozart and Haydn), then the Romantics (nineteenth century, the waltzes of Strauss, the ballets of Tchaikovsky) and finally to Contemporary music (twentieth century, represented here by John Cage). For this reason, the chapter is arranged chronologically, *not* in order of difficulty – you can ensure progression by reference to the 'Moving forward' section of each activity. There is a classical music time-line at the beginning of the chapter to show how the music used relates to other styles and composers. Supporting resource materials could be collected to set the music in the context of its time and culture. Choices of music other than the ones offered could be used; most of these activities can be easily adapted to other pieces. It is possible to explore classical music further through the activities in the *Listening* chapter, or investigate the use of classical music as a stimulus for composition with the activities 'Pavement café' and 'Composing with voices' on pages 31 and 37.

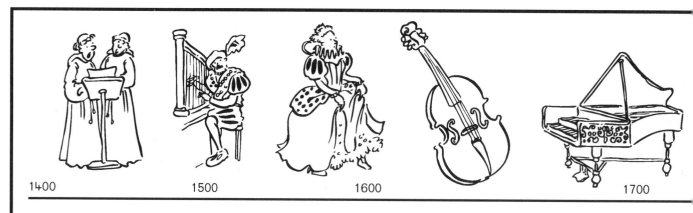

1400   1500   1600   1700

Church music	Henry VIII	Byrd (1543 – 1623)	Purcell (1659 – 1695)
Gregorian plainchant		Gibbons (1583 – 1625)	Vivaldi (1678 – 1750)
			Bach (1685 – 1750)

TUDOR PASTIMES

To develop awareness of the style of Tudor music.

†† *Whole class at the beginning of each session, then groups of four to six.*

🕐 *Two 45-minute sessions.*

🎵 *Session one: easy.*
    Session two: medium.

Previous skills/knowledge needed

The children need some experience of copying rhythmic patterns (as developed in 'Copy and Echo' on page 19), and to have done some singing. For session two, familiarity with using tuned and untuned instruments.

Key background information

Tudor music may be more familiar to you and the children than you realise: the song 'Greensleeves', thought to have been written by Henry VIII, is a very well-known Tudor tune, but the sounds and rhythms of Tudor instruments would also be familiar to the modern ear. Tudor music involved many instruments which we are familiar with today, such as drums, pipes (like our penny whistles), recorders, early trombones (called sackbuts), trumpets and violins, including the mechanical violin or hurdy-gurdy. At court, music followed the Royal fashion: Henry VII was not a lover of music, but both Henry VIII and Elizabeth I adored it. Henry VIII composed many tunes himself, and Elizabeth loved dancing. (Her particular favourite was the exciting new dance from Italy, 'La Volta,' in which the gentlemen lifted the ladies up by holding on to their wooden corsets.)

Vocabulary

Tudor, rhythm, consort of musicians.

Preparation

The example of Tudor music on the cassette that can be purchased to accompany this book, is another song thought to have been written by Henry VIII: 'Pastyme with Good Companye'. (You could use any recordings of Tudor music that are available in record stores and heritage shops – choose a piece with a strong rhythm). Listen to this song and try humming along with the tune, tapping the rhythm of the first half of the song. For session two, collect enough instruments for each child to have one. If you would like the children to write evaluations of their compositions or performances, make a copy of sheet 151 or sheet 152 for each group. Collect together any supporting resource materials to set the activity in a historical context (for example, paintings of the period, pictures of Tudor people and costume, videos of Tudor music or dance).

Resources needed

Recording of 'Pastyme with Good Companye' (from *English Madrigals and Songs* [Naxos]), or your own choice of music, cassette player, supporting resource materials. For session one: plain paper and writing materials. For session two: a combination of tuned and untuned instruments for each group of children (children could use their own instruments if they have them), one copy of photocopiable sheet 137 per group, one copy of sheet 151 or sheet 152 per group if required.

What to do
Session one

Tell the children some details about Tudor music (see 'Key background information'), showing them any supporting resource materials you have. Listen to the recording of 'Pastyme with Good Companye' together and explain to them that this song was thought to have been written by

Classical Music

1800   1900   2000

Haydn (1732 – 1809)   Wagner (1813 – 1883)   Copland (1900 – 1990)
  Mozart (1756 – 1791)   Debussy (1862 – 1918)   Cage (1912 – 1992)
    Beethoven (1770 – 1827)   Tchaikovsky (1873 – 1943)   Britten (1913 – 1976)
      Schubert (1797 – 1828)   Prokofiev (1891 – 1953)   Glass (born 1937)

Henry VIII. Play the recording through several times, inviting the children to hum along with the song and tapping your hands together on your knees in time with the rhythm of the tune. In the first half of the song, this rhythm is very easy to follow. It has a 1 – 2 – 3 – 4 pattern like this:

1	2	3	4	1	2	3	4	1	2	3	4	1	2	3	4
Pas	-	-	tyme	**with**	-	-	good	**co**	-o	-om	-pa	**nye**	-	-	I
1	2	3	4	1	2	3	4	1	2	3	4	1	2	3	4
lo	-o	-ve	and	**sha**	-a	-ll	un	-ti	-i	-l	l	**di**	-	-	-e

The pattern is the same with the next section:

> **Gruch** who **will** but **none** deny, so
> **God** be **pleased** so **live** will I.
> (*Gruch* = grumble/complain)

If you tap your hands on your knees on the **first** and **fourth** of every set of four beats, you will find that this follows the rhythm of the words themselves.

The pattern changes for the second half of the song. Ask the children to listen to the different rhythm in this part and to try tapping along with this too. The words are:

For my pastance hunt, sing and dance
My heart is set
All goodly sport for my comfort
Who shall me let?
(*pastance* = occupation/pastime)

When the children are humming (or singing) and tapping along with the tune comfortably, tell them that they are going to make up new verses to the song, following the same rhythm. Discuss possible themes for these verses: the song has already introduced the idea of leisure pursuits, so you might suggest the children continue with this theme. For example, they might write verses about dancing, drinking, hunting, reading, embroidery, or playing or listening to music. Alternatively, they might make the next verse a lament about how it feels when the 'good company' has gone away.

Give the groups fifteen to twenty minutes to work on their verses, stopping them once or twice to check on progress. They may find it quite hard to remember how the rhythm of the second half goes, if so, play the recording to them while they are working so that they can check whether or not their words fit in. Ask them to write their verses down so they do not forget them. Finish the session by asking each group to perform their new verse. It will help if you play the recording of the song quietly in the background as they sing, to remind them of the tune.

Session two

Start this session by reminding the children of the new verses they composed for 'Pastyme with Good Companye' in the first session, then tell them that each group is going to form a Royal Consort of Musicians. Their task will be to compose an instrumental accompaniment to the song to please His Majesty King Henry VIII. Stress that the accompaniment should be simple, and that it should follow the rhythm of the song. If they are playing tuned instruments, ask them to use the notes G, A, B and C only. Suggest that A would be a good note to start on, then they could try moving on to G. It might sound something like this, with the first of each set of four beats stressed:

```
1 2 3 4 1 2 3 4 1 2 3 4 1 2 3 4
A - - - A A - - - A G - - - G G - - - G
```

This pattern could be played on xylophones, chime bars, recorders or the children's own instruments. Untuned instruments (drums, tambours, tambourines) could be used to play the same pattern:

```
1 2 3 4 1 2 3 4 1 2 3 4 1 2 3 4
```

Give the groups about twenty-five minutes to develop and practise their accompaniments and to prepare a performance for the rest of the class. Play the recording repeatedly as they are working, so that they can check whether their notes and rhythms fit in with it. Give each group a Royal Consort sheet (sheet 137) and ask them to list the members of their consort and the names of their instruments. Ask them to write down the notes or rhythm of each instrument. They can do this in any way they choose, for example using note-

names, drawings or numbers. (See illustration). When all the groups have composed their accompaniments, bring them together to play them to each other. Play the recording along with each performance, and ask the rest of the class to evaluate how well each group kept in time with the song. Finish the session with each group first repeating its accompaniment along to the cassette, then singing the new verse they composed in session one. By this time, they should be able to sing their verse without the recording: ask them to try this and see how well they get on.

As a follow-up, you can ask the children to evaluate their composition or performance using sheets 151 or 152.

Suggestion(s) for extension

Children who have found it easy to compose a simple accompaniment can experiment with adding harmonies. It will help if they use a wider range of notes for this: for example, A and E together, followed by G and D together, would go well with the first part of the song.

Suggestion(s) for support

If some children are having difficulty internalising the rhythm of the words, encourage them to speak and clap them slowly at the same time. In session two, they can transfer the rhythm to an instrument, still speaking the words as they play.

Assessment opportunities

This activity provides opportunities for you to monitor the children's developing awareness of different musical styles, their ability to hold a rhythm in their heads and keep in time with each other and their skills in playing and composing with instruments.

Opportunities for IT

A background rhythm can be programmed into a keyboard or computer and played along with the children's compositions to help keep a steady beat; this will also add an extra instrumental sound to each consort.

Display ideas

The completed consort sheets and evaluation sheets (if you have used them) can be displayed along with language and art work relating to the Tudors. Some of the instruments the children have used can be put on display with the recording of the song. Those viewing the display can be invited to play the rhythms and notes from the consort sheets while listening to the recording.

Reference to photocopiable sheets

Sheet 137 identifies some of the instruments used in Tudor times and invites the children to list the instruments used in their own Royal Consort of Musicians. Sheet 151 is a composition evaluation sheet. Sheet 152 invites children to evaluate their performances.

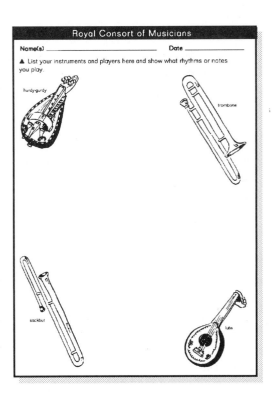

Moving forward

This activity links well with 'Performance poetry' on page 34 and 'Chartbusters' on page 94 as both activities emphasise the rhythm of words. There is also an interesting link with 'Composing with voices' on page 37 which offers the opportunity to compare the secular music used here with the sacred music of Tudor times. The children could use the rhythms they have explored in this activity as a basis for making up their own Tudor-style dances. The rhythm would go particularly well with the 'step-hop' movement characteristic of dances of the time.

BASIC BAROQUE

To introduce children to the principal features of Baroque music and to develop their listening skills.

♯♯ *Whole class, working in two groups.*

🕐 *Three 20-minute sessions.*

🎵 *Medium.*

Previous skills/knowledge needed

The children need to have some experience of listening to and discussing music. The vocabulary development activities in 'Talking about music' on page 40 could be used for this, as could 'Telling tales: music for ballet' on page 62. 'Instrument actions' in the *Listening* chapter of the Key Stage 1 book would also be a good preparation for this activity, as it makes similar use of mime to represent instruments being played.

Key background information

Whether we realise it or not, most of us are familiar with a number of examples of baroque music, such as those from films, advertisements, the doctor's waiting room or the supermarket aisles. Handel's *Water Music*, Vivaldi's *Four Seasons* and Bach's *Air on a G String* are so widely known that, although many of us might find it difficult to say which was which, we could probably hum along to them if they came on the radio. The work of Purcell, though less widely known, will also be familiar to many people.

One of the most distinctive features of baroque music is its instrumentation, and this is the focus of the activity. Many of the instruments used in modern symphony orchestras either did not exist at all or existed in earlier forms during the baroque period: brass instruments, for example, were simpler and much harder to play, which restricted the sort of performance composers could expect these instruments to give. Perhaps the most distinctive instrument of all was the harpsichord, which was joined by stringed instruments, woodwind and brass to form the chamber music 'ensemble'. One of the low-pitched instruments – often a 'cello or a close relative called the violone – would play the *continuo*: this was a bass line played (as its name suggests) continuously throughout the piece.

Vocabulary

Baroque, harpsichord, ensemble, solo, continuo.

Preparation

Before session one, listen two or three times to the extract from the first movement of Bach's *Brandenburg Concerto no. 2* (the first one and a half minutes), available on the cassette. Do the same with the beginning of the second movement before session two. Each time, listen carefully to the instruments used; this may seem difficult at first, but listen again and it will become easier to distinguish them.

For session two, make one copy of the 'musical comparisons' sheet 133 for each child, if required. For session three, make one copy of the analysis sheet 138 for each child and an additional copy enlarged onto A3 paper.

Resources needed

Recording of extracts from the first and second movements of Bach's *Brandenburg Concerto no. 2* (Naxos), or your own version, cassette player, one copy of photocopiable sheet 138 for each child and one copy enlarged to A3, one copy of photocopiable sheet 133 if required.

What to do

Session one

Play the excerpt from the first movement to the children, telling them what it is. Ask whether they can work out what instruments are playing. They will probably recognise violins, a trumpet and a recorder, but they may have more difficulty identifying the oboe, the 'cello and the harpsichord.

Set half the class out as an imaginary instrumental ensemble (see diagram below) with the harpsichord player facing the rest of the ensemble in order to direct them. The exact size and composition of the ensemble will depend upon the number of children, but the essential instruments are one each of: trumpet, recorder, oboe, violin, harpsichord and one or two 'cellos. The remainder of the group should consist of a group of violins which will play when the whole ensemble is playing, but not during the violin solos. The ensemble should constitute half the class in total.

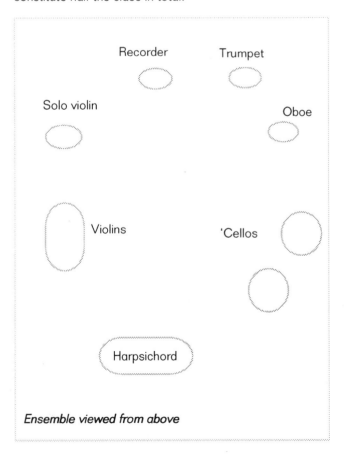

Ensemble viewed from above

Explain to the children that they have to position themselves and their hands to look as though they are really playing the instruments. Seat the other half of the class as an audience. Ask them to watch the 'performance' carefully and to note whether or not the instrumentalists are playing at the right time. Play the recording a second time for everyone to listen to, pointing out the different instruments as they are heard (the oboe is the hardest to hear). Then play it again, this time asking each 'instrumentalist' to imitate the playing of their counterpart on the recording. It does not matter whether or not they are able to follow the pattern of the tune, but they should only pretend to play when their instrument is actually playing on the recording. Repeat this

take turns to play; the 'cellos should be able to describe their continuous part (the *continuo*); the violins should know that there are times when they all play together and times when they do not play at all.

Conclude this first session by listening to the excerpt again, bearing in mind the points you have discussed. Alternatively, you might prefer to listen to the whole of this movement (if you have your own recording), now that the children have some idea of how it is put together.

Session two

This session follows exactly the same format as session one, except that it uses an excerpt from the second

two or three times, reminding the 'audience' to watch and listen quietly.

At first, the children will probably try to play all the time, but by the second or third time through, they should be developing an awareness of their own part, and be able to anticipate some of their entries – for example, the trumpet soloist should be ready to play the high solo very near the beginning of the piece, and again towards the end of the extract.

Discuss the performance with the 'audience': were the players giving an accurate representation of the music? Ask the instrumentalists to explain their own parts, and how they fit into the piece. For example, the trumpet player might be able to tell you about his or her very high solos; the harpsichord player should be able to tell you that he or she plays all the way through; the recorder, oboe and violin soloists might describe the way in which their instruments

movement (the slow movement) of the concerto, and uses the 'audience' half of the class as instrumentalists (the original instrumentalists now become the audience).

Features to look out for in this movement are its slowness in comparison with the first movement, and the fact that there is only one of each instrument playing with no trumpet part at all. As a result, there are only five players in this movement, so to accommodate your half-class performers, it is suggested that you assign the solo violin, recorder and oboe parts to single children, and ask the rest of the group to represent either 'cello or harpsichord players. Ask the 'instrumentalists' to perform the second extract as in session one, with the 'audience' commenting on what they hear. To conclude this session, play both excerpts (or both whole movements) and ask the class to listen for the differences between the two. You could ask them to write down their observations using photocopiable sheet 133.

Session three

Start this session by briefly repeating the instrumental imitations from sessions one and two to remind the children of the music, then give out the analysis sheet 138. Decide whether to focus on the first or second movement for your analysis. Ask them to listen very carefully while you play the recording and to chart the part of *one* instrument (or instrument group) as they listen. They can do this either by simply drawing a horizontal line when the instrument is playing, and breaking the line when it stops, or by using their own informal notation (see the *Notation* chapter for ideas). Make sure that all the instruments in the piece are represented across the class as a whole.

Play the excerpt three or four times through (or more if necessary) then compare the children's charts. Ask the class to decide which is the most accurate for each instrument and why. As a follow-up, the children can transfer the most accurate charts onto the enlarged A3 copy for display. Finally, discuss the features of Baroque music which they have discovered and listen to the music one more time. (These features could be described in writing to add to a class display – see 'Display ideas'.)

Suggestion(s) for support

If the class are finding it very hard to distinguish the different instrumental sounds within a piece of music, you could all focus on one instrument only (for example, the trumpet in the first movement, and the solo violin or oboe in the second), and try and notice exactly what it does and when.

Assessment opportunities

This activity enables you to assess the children's growing awareness of different styles of music, their ability to listen carefully, to identify instruments and to represent their sounds using informal notation.

Suggestion(s) for extension

Children who have shown skill in listening and analysing during these sessions can use the analysis sheets independently to listen to and analyse other examples of baroque music. Alternatively, they could listen to music of another period and devise and use appropriate analysis sheets for this, according to the instruments used.

Opportunities for IT

The children could use an art or drawing package to create their own analysis sheets. They could draw a coloured line for each of the instruments when it is playing and then experiment by changing the thickness or variations of a dotted line to represent the volume or speed that the instrument is playing. To do this the children will need to

know how to draw lines and use the menus to change the style, colour or thickness of the line.

These analysis sheets could be printed out for class display, possibly alongside a word-processed description of the music or information about instruments taken from a CD-ROM encyclopaedia such as Microsoft's *Musical Instruments*.

Display ideas
The analysis sheets can be displayed with written descriptions of the music, and pictures of instruments from the period. You could also demonstrate the link between Baroque styles in music and in architecture by displaying pictures of Baroque instruments alongside pictures of baroque buildings.

Reference to photocopiable sheets
Photocopiable sheet 138 provides a format for analysing the instrumentation used in baroque music. This format could easily be adapted for other musical styles. Sheet 133 invites the children to compare two pieces of music, in this case, the first and second movements of Bach's Brandenburg Concerto no 2.

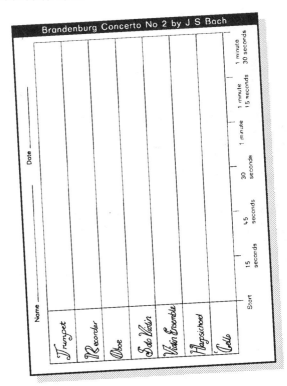

Moving forward
It is a good idea to repeat this activity using other examples of music from the same period. You could then compare these with other types of music using 'The style game' on page 46. You might like to compare baroque music with that of the Tudors using 'Tudor pastimes' in this chapter. 'Pattern tracking' on page 96 provides further opportunities to analyse musical structure.

JUMPED UP MOZART

To develop awareness of the style of Mozart and the concept of arpeggios.
†† *Whole class, then small groups of four or five.*
🕐 *Two 55-minute sessions.*
🎵 *Medium.*

Previous skills/knowledge needed
This activity requires dexterity on the whistle and xylophone. 'Introducing scales' on page 23 asks the children to play scales on these instruments. 'Stars in your eyes' on page 106 introduces the concept of grid notation which is used extensively in this activity.

Key background information
Mozart is one of the most important composers in the Classical period. He was born in Salzburg (1756) and died in Vienna at the age of 35. As a child he was a prodigy, playing in specially-organised concerts from the age of six. He went to Vienna where he was presented to the Emperor who was a keen lover of the baroque style of music. Mozart's music was considered modern and sometimes rather risqué as it used new instruments, such as the clarinet, and less formalised tunes. He composed many symphonies, works for orchestras and concertos. He uses both scales and arpeggios extensively in his music. 'Queen of the Night's Aria' (song) is full of arpeggios which are sung so high that the singer has to use a special tone of voice to sing it. Other well-known works are *Eine Kleine Nachtmusik* ('a little night music') which has arpeggios right at the beginning of the piece, and the *Clarinet Concerto* which is full of beautiful, although heart-rending, tunes. An arpeggio is a set of musical jumps as shown below.

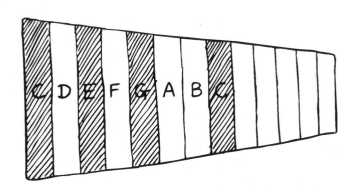

Vocabulary
Symphony, concerto, aria (a song sung in an opera), the Classical period (Classical as different from Romantic or Baroque music), arpeggios.

Preparation

Listen to 'Queen of the Night's Aria' and the beginning of *Eine Kleine Nachtmusik*, both extracts are available on the cassette. Collect together enough chime bars or xylophones/glockenspiels for one per group (see 'Resources needed'), and arrange them in the room so that the groups can seat themselves round them comfortably.

Resources needed

Glockenspiels/xylophones containing notes C, E, G, C and G, B, D, a set of chime bars – set one needs C, E, G, C' (or high C), set two needs G, B, D, G' (or high G), obviously the G can be used jointly by both sets – one beater for each group, writing materials, cassette player, recordings of Mozart's 'Queen of the Night's Aria' from *The Magic Flute* and the first movement of *Eine Kleine Nachtmusik* (Naxos), or your own versions, one blank cassette, one copy of photocopiable sheet 143 for each group and one copy of sheet 133 for each child.

What to do

Session one

Introduce the idea of an *arpeggio*. Demonstrate the sound, using set one of the chime bars (C, E, G, C') for arpeggio one and set two (G, B, D, G') for the second arpeggio. Ask the class to sing up and down the arpeggios as you play the chime bars. Divide the class into groups and ask them to sit round an instrument and number themselves one to four/five. Ask all the number ones to play the first arpeggio, one after another, then all the number twos and so on. Repeat the process with the second arpeggio.

Go round the class, playing again. This time each player can choose whether they play arpeggio one or two, and if they want to go up or down. Do this without interruption until everyone has played twice. Ask the children to listen to the arpeggios they have played and decide which combination of the scales and arpeggios they think sounds best.

Now ask the children to do exactly the same thing round their own group, passing the beater from player to player. This will form their group composition. Give them four minutes to work on their compositions. Ask them to think up symbols to represent arpeggio one, going up or down, and arpeggio two, going up or down. If the children are familiar with grid notation they can use it to write down their composition. If the children have not used this method of notation you may wish to end the session at this point and plan one using the activity 'Stars in your eyes' on page 106 to teach grid notation.

Give each group a copy of photocopiable sheet 143 and ask them to notate their work by writing one arpeggio symbol in each square of the grid.

Give the groups five minutes to write this down and practise it (although this sounds a very short time the children often work better in short intensive bursts with a clear goal at the end). Now tell them that they have two minutes to practise what they have written down before they perform it to the class. Often, giving young children several opportunities for intensive practice, rather than a single long session, helps them to stay on task. It also gives the teacher the opportunity to comment on 'good practice' seen or points that can be worked on. Suggest that two children play the arpeggios, one acts as the pointer, one listens particularly carefully to see how it can be improved and one introduces it (if there are only four in the group the latter could introduce and point). Let each group play through their piece once before ending the session.

Session two

Start the session by asking each group to remind themselves of their composition and prepare to play it to the class. This time they could use different people to perform the various tasks.

When they have heard each other's music tell them that you are going to play them two pieces of music that use arpeggios. Ask the children to listen quietly first. Play them the opening of *Eine Kleine Nachtmusik*. Play it two or three times, asking them to listen for all the arpeggios they can hear. Next, play the 'Queen of the Night's Aria'. Explain that the singer is singing in a very special way so that she can sing high notes.

Give a copy of sheet 133 to each child. Divide the class in half, keeping them in their groups. Tell one half that they are going to listen to and write about the first piece of music and that the other half will do the same with the second piece. Use open and closed questions such as:

▲ Does it start with arpeggios?
▲ How many arpeggios could they count?
▲ Does it start quietly or loudly?
▲ Is it fast or slow?
▲ Does it repeat any part of it?
▲ Does it start with all the instruments or do some come in later on?
▲ Which is their favourite part?
▲ What does the music do when it is not an arpeggio?
▲ Are the notes next door to one another or are they in huge jumps?

Give them time to write down some opinions on the sheet. Then ask them to think about and compare this music with their own compositions, and write comparisons on the sheet. Play the two Mozart pieces one more time and give the children time to discuss and complete the sheet. As a grand finale play all the music, both Mozart's and the class's compositions, and record the latter.

Suggestion(s) for extension

If the whole class or a particular group appear very confident, ask them to add in a third arpeggio: D, F sharp (black metal), A, D and write a new piece incorporating this. They might find they need two grids for a longer piece. Ask the group to practise their composition, playing it at the same speed as is on the recording they listened to. Give them the recording to listen to again and see if they make up a piece that sounds similar in style.

Suggestion(s) for support

If the class are finding it hard, you might need to go back to reinforce the basic skills of playing an arpeggio, before coming back to this lesson. If individuals are finding it difficult, suggest that they play only three-note arpeggios. These would be played more slowly to fit in with the pulse of the grid.

Assessment opportunities

This activity gives the opportunity to assess children's skill in using arpeggios, notating their own compositions and awareness of the style of music from another time.

Opportunities for IT

The children could use software such as *Music Box, Music*

Explorer or *Miracle Piano* to research and practise other arpeggios. The children could also use a drawing package to notate their finished arpeggios.

Display ideas

Use the photocopiable sheet 143 as a basis for display. Put the comparison sheet 133 about the other two pieces of music alongside them. Have the recordings, both of the Mozart music and the children's compositions, displayed with the cassette player so that observers can hear and make their own judgements.

Reference to photocopiable sheets

Sheet 143 is a grid notation sheet which the children use to record their compositions. Sheet 133 invites children to compare two pieces of music. (This can be used for any listening activity.)

Moving forward

If you wish to compose more music in the style of a period or culture, use 'Waltzing Victorians' in this chapter, 'Chinese whispers' and 'Recreating a raga' on pages 78 and 86. The first two activities use xylophones as a major focus. If you wish to explore Mozart's music further, the *Listening* chapter suggests many different ways to do this.

TELLING TALES: MUSIC FOR BALLET

To develop children's awareness of the narrative use of music, and of different musical styles and techniques.

♯♯ *Whole class, working in pairs.*

🕐 *45 minutes for each option.*

♫ *Option one: easy.*
    Options two and three: medium.

Previous skills/knowledge needed

The children need to have some experience of listening carefully to music. The music vocabulary activities in 'Talking about music' on page 40 would be useful for this. The activity 'Zein's tune' on page 74 also offers opportunities for analytical listening.

Key background information

Music for ballet as we think of it today did not really come into its own until the nineteenth century. Prior to this, although dances were included in operatic productions (for example, by Purcell in the seventeenth century and by Gluck in the eighteenth century), they were merely entertaining interludes and did not carry the force of the plot. The ballets we will be considering here, however, tell their stories entirely through dance. The first is Prokofiev's *Romeo and Juliet*, and the second is Tchaikovsky's *Swan Lake*. Both of these ballets are love stories and, in both, the story ends with the lovers being tragically united in death. The cassette includes short excerpts from each, but you may prefer to use your own recordings.

This activity offers three different ways in which children can explore how stories can be conveyed through music:

▲ Option one – asks the children 'What do *you* think is happening?' in the music;

▲ Option two – involves comparing one piece of music with the other;

▲ Option three – invites the children to plan an imaginary ballet of their own.

You can use all three options if you wish, or just follow one or two.

Vocabulary

Ballet, romantic, tragic, threatening and so on, dynamics (volume), instrumentation, Prokofiev, Tchaikovsky.

Preparation

Listen to the two pieces of music so that you are familiar with them. Make one copy of the photocopiable sheet appropriate to the option you have chosen (see reference to photocopiable sheets) for each child.

Resources needed

Recordings of excerpts from 'Montagues and Capulets' from *Romeo and Juliet* by Prokofiev and the final scene from *Swan Lake* by Tchaikovsky (Naxos), or your own version, cassette player, one copy of the appropriate photocopiable sheet for each child, writing and colouring materials.

What to do

Option one

Give out a copy of sheet 132 to each child. Group the children in pairs and tell them that you are going to play two pieces of ballet music (but do not tell them the titles). Play them 'Montagues and Capulets' two or three times and ask them to discuss with their partners what they think is happening in the music, then jot down some ideas and sketches on one of their sheets. Do the same with the final scene from *Swan Lake*, asking the children to put their ideas and sketches for this on their second sheet. Remember that this is a listening activity, not an English one. The children can use written notes or drawings, or a combination of both –

whichever they feel most comfortable with. Ask each pair to compare their ideas with another pair: did they guess the same thing? Compare guesses across the class: did everyone think the same things were happening? (Emphasise that, although each composer was trying to convey a specific story, the children's own interpretations are just as valid.) They might have felt there was an element of strength or anger in the first piece, or the sound of marching feet. The second piece might have suggested a feeling of restlessness, then a pursuit, followed by some sort of threatening triumph. If so, what was it about the music that made them think this? If not, what events did the music suggest to them? Can they explain why?

Identify the two pieces of music. Explain that the first (*Romeo and Juliet*) depicts the rivalry of members of two feuding families, while the second (*Swan Lake*) depicts the story of a princess turned into a swan by an evil sorcerer. Ask the class to listen to the extracts again, now that they know the composers' intentions. How successful do they feel the composers have been? Discuss what other sounds or effects the composers might have used to put their stories across – for example, if they were writing ballet music today. The children might also consider the way in which film music portrays events and atmosphere, and compare this with the ballet music.

Complete the session by asking each half of the class (or smaller groups) to mime a scene, either from the original ballet story or their own version, while you play one of the recordings. This could be then extended into dance and/or drama lessons.

Option two

Give out a copy of sheet 133 to each child. Tell them that they are going to hear two pieces of ballet music, and tell them what they are about. Ask the children to write the titles and composers of the two pieces onto their sheets. Now ask them to work in pairs, listening carefully to each piece of

music, discussing it and writing notes on *one* of their two sheets about what they have heard. For example, they might write 'loud' or 'quiet', 'strong rhythm', 'restless', 'violins' or 'lots of low notes'. Play the two pieces of music, pausing between them to give the children time to talk and write. Play the music again, asking them to add anything they feel is missing to their sheets.

Now ask the pairs to look at their notes and, using two colours, draw a line of one colour to join up any features that are the *same* in both pieces of music, and a line of a different colour to join up any features that are *different* (for example, 'loud' and 'quiet', or 'strong, steady beat' and 'uneven rhythm'). Play the two extracts again to help clarify these points.

Now ask each pair to use their second sheet to write up their notes into a series of statements describing each piece of music, using the same colours as before to join similar and different features of the music. For example, they might write: 'Prokofiev uses loud sounds to show the families are angry' and join it to 'Tchaikovsky uses loud sounds to show the sorcerer is angry' to indicate similarity, and write:

Classical Music

'"Montagues and Capulets" has a strong steady beat' and join it to 'The final scene from *Swan Lake* has an uneven rhythm which makes the music feel restless' to show difference. If this makes too many demands on their writing skills, the children could just list similarities and differences, for example:

Prokofiev   *Tchaikovsky*
loud sounds = angry family   loud sounds = angry sorcerer

Finally, compare the statements across the class, discussing different children's ideas.

Option three

Play the two ballet pieces to the children and discuss how the composers tell the stories with music. (If you have done options one and two of this activity, remind the children of the features they have already discussed.) Ask them to think in particular about the way the composers use the instruments and changes in volume (dynamics) to create certain effects. Now ask the children to imagine that they have been commissioned to write the music for a ballet based on a story of their choice and using any instruments or sounds they like. Give a copy of sheet 139 to each child and ask them to work in pairs to plan their ballet following the guidelines on the sheet. They could use one of the two sheets to brainstorm ideas and possibilities, and the other to write up their final decisions. Point out to the children that they can plan to use any instruments or sounds; they do not have to be able to play them themselves. Conclude the session by asking each pair to describe and explain their plan to the rest of the class.

Suggestion(s) for extension

Children who have responded well to these activities can listen to a range of music from other ballets and use this to devise a ballet story of their own. They can record extracts from the ballets into a sequence of their own choice and perhaps devise dance movements to go with it.

The children could use videos of films and ballets to investigate the way that music contributes to the telling of the story. (Extension to option one).

Suggestion(s) for support

Some children will find it very hard to describe what they can hear in a piece of music. It will help if you ask them to concentrate on just one feature, such as dynamics (volume) or instrumentation.

Assessment opportunities

This activity will enable you to monitor children's awareness of different musical styles and techniques and the way in which these can be used to create certain effects. You will also be able to assess their ability to listen with concentration, to describe music using appropriate vocabulary and to respond to it in a variety of ways.

Opportunities for IT

The children could use a word processor or desktop publishing package to write up the notes in session two into a series of statements which can then be linked using different-coloured lines. The children or the teacher can set up a page with two columns and a gap between them. The children's statements can be fitted into the columns (see diagram below).

Display ideas

All the sheets used in this activity can be used for display, accompanied by pictures of ballet scenes and synopses of the stories.

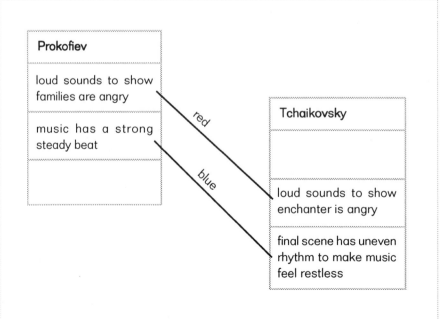

Reference to photocopiable sheets

Sheet 132 invites the children to describe what they think is happening in the music. Sheet 133 offers a framework for comparing two pieces of music. Sheet 139 asks the children to plan music for a ballet based on a story of their choice.

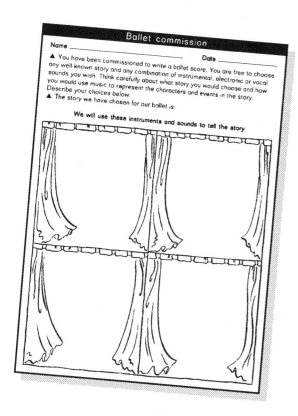

Moving forward

This activity can be repeated using any other ballet music or 'programme music' (music which depicts a certain scene or event, like 'Fingal's Cave' by Mendelssohn). It also links well with the activities in the *Listening* chapter, particularly 'How do they do that?' in 'Talking about music' on page 40 uses sheet 134 which invites children to focus on how a composer uses the effects of dynamics, timbre or texture. 'Journey line' on page 44 also links well with this activity, as it focuses on the sequence of events in a piece of music.

WALTZING VICTORIANS

To introduce and experience the style of waltz music.

†† *Whole class in groups of two or three.*

🕐 *55 minutes.*

🎵 *Medium.*

Previous skills/knowledge needed

For this activity the children need to know how to play the xylophone and read grid notation. 'Introducing scales' on page 23 teaches scales through the use of xylophones. 'Stars in your eyes' on page 106 introduces grid notation.

Key background information

The waltz is a dance using a beat of 1, 2, 3, 1, 2, 3, **1**, 2, 3, 1, 2, 3. It is thought to have originated from the Austrian folk dance the 'Ländler'. The music used in the film *The Sound of Music,* when Maria dances with Captain Von Trapp, is an example of this, as is the 'Oom, pah, pah' song in the musical *Oliver.* From about 1790 onwards, the dance became incorporated into 'polite' European society. Many Romantic classical composers wrote in waltz time: Chopin's *The Minute Waltz*, Weber's *Invitation to the Dance*, Tchaikovsky's *Serenade for Strings* and Ravel's *La Valse*. However, the most prolific and popular composers using the waltz as dance music were the Strauss family, particularly the younger Johann Strauss who worked in Vienna. In England, at first, the Victorians thought the waltz was conducive to lasciviousness and immorality, and highly unsuitable for young ladies. The basis of a waltz is the continuous 'um, pa, pa, um, pa, pa' rhythm that is kept going in the bass instruments. This rhythm uses a very simple combination of chords and these chords are what the composition in this activity will be based on.

Vocabulary
Chord, waltz time.

Preparation
Before the session you may wish to listen to one of Strauss's waltzes to become familiar with the rhythm. The *Blue Danube Waltz* is provided on the cassette. Tap the rhythm as the piece plays. Collect sets of chime bars and xylophones containing the notes C, D, E, G, B and a high D. If you wish, you could put colour-coded stickers onto the bars, so that all the C chord notes are one colour (C, E, G), and all the G chord notes another (G, B, D). Obviously the G will have two stickers. Make one enlarged copy of photocopiable page 140 and enough copies for one per two children in the class. Before the session you may wish to practise playing a chord on the xylophone in the way outlined in the activity.

Resources needed
The notes C, D, E, G, B and a high D on xylophone and chime bars, glockenspiels and any other tuned instruments you might have available, three beaters per set of notes, one enlarged photocopiable sheet 140 and enough copies of the same sheet for one between two children, recording of *The Blue Danube* (Naxos), or any Strauss waltz.

What to do
Listen to a Strauss waltz with the class. Draw attention to the 1, 2, 3 rhythm and ask them to tap along with it, counting 1, 2, 3 in their heads, if necessary. Using one xylophone, demonstrate how the 1, 2, 3 can be transferred onto an instrument. Arrange the children so there are two or three children to a xylophone (you could use three beaters to an instrument if you wish).

Show the class how the notes are arranged on instruments: play one, miss one, play one. This arrangement of three notes is a *chord*. Make it clear that you can have different chords using different notes but the arrangement of the notes would still be roughly the same.

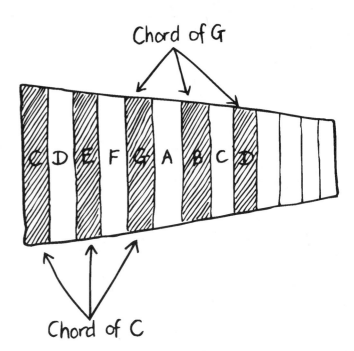

To make the 'um, pa, pa' rhythm, play the C first with one beater (to make the 'um') then the E and G at the same time using the other two beaters together to create the 'pa, pa' effect. These notes form a *C chord*, or chord of C.

Let the whole group practise by all saying 'um, pa, pa' and just miming their beater movements at the correct time without actually playing the instrument. Then play the notes of C chord in the 'um, pa, pa' form. When the children are accustomed to doing this, introduce the idea of playing the 'um, pa, pa' sequence four times without a break. Starting together is difficult as is playing at the same pace, and the children will need to practise this as a whole group.

The use of simple notations can be introduced at this point. Using the enlarged photocopiable sheet 140, ask one child to stand beside the music. For each 'um' or 'pa' they must point to a letter or symbol, reading the sheet left to right and line by line, as they would read a book. Read only the first line of the (chord) music at this stage.

When the children are confident with this process introduce the chord of G. For this they will need G, B, D. Repeat the previous process but this time read the second line of (chord) music from the sheet. When the children are confident with this part try playing the whole sheet without stopping. They have now got the outline, structure and sound for the bass line of a simple waltz. Give each group of two to three children a copy of sheet 140.

To create a tune to play over the top of this bass line, ask

a group (approximately a quarter of the class) of children to continue using the 'um, pa, pa' rhythm but to play their own choice of notes, choosing from the notes written in the appropriate places on the music sheet. They can put these notes in any order they like, but they must choose from the notes that go with each 'um, pa, pa' section of the bass line. These notes should be played on the higher sounding instruments if possible – a recorder, penny whistle or higher sounding xylophone are ideal.

When the children have had a chance to practise and try out their ideas put the two parts together and play the world premiere of the ... Waltz!

Suggestion(s) for extension

Ask the children to try out a tune that does not use the 'um, pa, pa' rhythm but uses faster running notes, provided they still fit in with the beat of the 'um, pa, pa' bass line.

Let the children experiment with introducing an F chord (F A C) to the bass line where it is indicated on the music sheet with a ♣ (this will replace the C chord). The tune over the top could also be changed at this point.

Suggestion(s) for support

If all the children are finding the activity difficult, practise playing the chords slowly while the group who played the tune say 'um, pa, pa'. If an individual child is finding it hard, ask her or him to play the 'um' part of the chord on a single chime bar.

Assessment opportunities

This activity gives good opportunities for assessing the children's awareness of different styles of music, whether they can play in time with each other, hold a part by themselves, play with each other, have an awareness of using notations and also the level of their co-ordination when handling beaters.

Opportunities for IT

The children could set up the bass line chords using a keyboard. The bass line could be set to play continuously while the children compose the treble line for the tune of the waltz. The final composition could be recorded using the memory of the keyboard or transferred to the computer using

a MIDI interface. In the latter case, the music could be imported into a notation package such as Longman's *Notation* and scored using traditional music notation.

The children could also experiment with chords using software such as *Music Explorer* or *Music Box*. The final chords can be used as the bass line for the children's own waltz compositions using the tune maker part of the software.

Display ideas

To get the idea of the excitement, magic and romance of the waltz, draw or paint waltzing figures in Victorian ball gowns. Contemporary Victorian pictures could be used to research suitable costumes and stance: for example, James Tissot's painting (1873) entitled *Too Early* shows a ballroom scene which would be a useful focus for discussion. This puts the music in the context of its time and gives an alternative perspective to the Disney world of *Sleeping Beauty*.

Reference to photocopiable sheet

Sheet 140 sets out the chords and notes required to play a simple waltz, using grid notation.

Moving forward

If you want to explore the idea of composing in a particular style 'Tudor pastimes' and 'Jumped up Mozart' on pages 52 and 59 together with 'Chinese whispers' and 'Sleeping angels' on pages 78 and 83, would provide support.

SOUND CAGE

To develop awareness of contemporary experimental music through listening and composition.

†† *Whole class, then groups of four to six.*

⏱ *Session one: 45 minutes.*
Session two: 60 minutes.

♫ *Advanced.*

Previous skills/knowledge needed

The children will need to be fairly confident in using tuned and untuned percussion and in exploring instrumental sounds. They will need to be able to keep a steady beat and to hold a rhythmic pattern independently of others. As the music on which this activity is based is influenced by the rhythms and sounds of South-East Asia, 'Sleeping angels' on page 83 would be a particularly good preparation. 'African polyrhythms' on page 80 would also provide useful experience of combining different rhythms. The idea of contrasting sound with silence is important in this activity; for this reason it would be a good idea to revisit 'Creating silence' on page 18.

Key background information

This activity uses the music of John Cage (1912 – 1992) as a starting-point. Cage is probably one of the most famous of this century's experimental composers, along with Schoenberg, under whom he studied from 1935 to 1937. Cage was an outspoken member of the avant-garde arts movement during the 1930s and 1940s. He rejected the Western classical tradition in music, stressing instead the importance of rhythm and percussion sounds, and drawing on non-Western styles (for example, the Balinese gamelan) for inspiration. His most famous (or infamous) piece, composed in 1952, consists of 4 minutes 33 seconds of silence. He was also very interested in composing by chance: for example, his 'Music of Changes' (1951) was composed by tossing a coin. The piece used here was composed in 1940, and is one of a series based on Balinese rhythms. If you do not have the cassette, other pieces by Cage could be used, or any modern experimental piece which explores a range of sounds and has a strong rhythm.

Vocabulary

Experimental, rhythm, timbre, improvise, compose.

Preparation

Listen to the extract from John Cage's 'Second Construction' on the cassette, noting the way in which each new rhythm takes over from the last. Try counting in eights as you listen, noticing how each rhythmic pattern fits into the count. For session one, you do not need any instruments. For session two, collect enough tuned and untuned instruments (including improvised instruments made of junk, items from home or the classroom) for each group to have a plenty of choice.

Resources needed

Session one: cassette player and blank cassette (optional). Session two: recording of 'Second Construction' by John Cage (from *Works for Percussion* [Wergo]), or your own choice of music, cassette player, blank cassette (optional), enough tuned and untuned instruments for each group, paper.

What to do

Session one

Sit in a circle with the children and ask them to close their eyes. Tell them you are going to do a rhythmic improvisation together, with each person trying out different rhythmic patterns with hands and bodies. Start the improvisation yourself with a simple pattern. For example, you might create a pattern like this, using hands on knees:

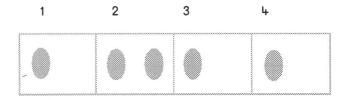

Repeat this pattern a few times, but *leave a gap* between each pattern. You do not have to count a set number of beats in the gap: it can be a different length each time. When you have done this a few times, invite the children to try

their own 4-beat rhythmic patterns using hands and knees. Ask them to 'play' their rhythms *in the gaps*, so that one pattern takes over from another. Keep interspersing your rhythms with the children's. Continue with this for a couple of minutes, so that the children really get used to listening for the silences. Ask them to try out different rhythmic patterns, perhaps trying some more complex ideas.

For example, they might stretch their patterns out over more beats:

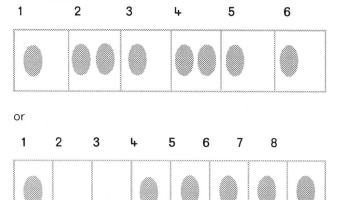

or

If you have done 'African polyrhythms' on page 80 with the children, you might like to suggest that they invent rhythms to fit into 5, 7 or 9 beats. For example:

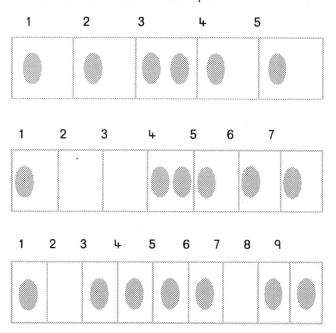

If you do not feel confident about doing something as complex as this, keep to simple rhythms and concentrate on listening to the silences – this activity works equally well with very simple patterns.

Once you are all comfortable with your rhythmic patterns and have tried out a few possibilities, start to introduce voice sounds into them along with or instead of the hand and body sounds. You do not need to use singing voices – squeaks, growls, grunts and hoots will do equally well. Practise this in the same way as you did with the hand and body sounds,

trying out a range of possibilities and still listening out for the silences.

To conclude this session, split the class into groups of four to six and ask them to develop their own rhythmic improvisation using hands, bodies and voices in the way you have been doing as a whole class. Give them about 10 minutes to work on their ideas then ask them to present them to the rest of the class. (Remind the children that they do not have to present a finished composition; they are just

sharing their ideas in an improvisation.) Record these if possible, for use in session two.

Session two

If you have recorded the group improvisations from session one, start this session by playing them, discussing the sounds you can hear, and the way in which each pattern follows on from the last. Go straight into a whole-class rhythmic improvisation, listening for the silences and using a combination of hand, voice and body sounds.

Now listen to the extract from John Cage's 'Second

Construction' (or your own choice of music), and ask the children to notice the way in which the different rhythmic patterns follow on from one another. (If they have done 'Sleeping Angels' on page 83, they may notice the similarity between this music and that of South-East Asia.) When they have listened to the extract once, point out that in Cage's piece, the different patterns sometimes interrupt each other. Play the extract again, asking the children to listen to the way that many of the patterns emerge out of the background,

get louder, then disappear again. (This could be compared with an image floating to the foreground of a film or pop video then gradually receding.)

Start a new rhythmic improvisation with the class, this time asking the children to try to make their rhythmic patterns emerge and recede in the same way as John Cage does in his piece. Invite the children to interrupt each other this time, rather than waiting for a silence before beginning. Try this two or three times, with different rhythms and combinations of sounds.

When you are comfortable with this new improvisation, divide the class into the same groups as for session one and tell them that they are going to make up their own rhythmic compositions for instruments. Stress that this time, after exploring their ideas through *improvisation*, they are going to create a *composition* which can be remembered and repeated. Listen to 'Second Construction' one more time, asking the children to focus on the instrument sounds used. They may have difficulty recognising the instruments as many of the rhythms are played on a 'prepared piano' which has had the timbre or sound-quality of its notes deliberately altered, while other sounds are made by striking or shaking a sheet of metal. More recognisable sounds are made by a snare drum, a glockenspiel and a shaker. Ask the children to think about the instrument sounds they would like to include in their compositions, and about how these might be produced.

Give each group a range of tuned and untuned instruments (including improvised instruments) and ask them to try out some ideas through improvisation for ten minutes or so. Stop the class, listen to some of the groups' ideas and discuss them, then give each group a piece of paper and ask them to create their composition, writing it down in any way they choose, as long as it helps them to remember how the music goes. They can use words, pictures or any type of formal or informal notation. Ask them to bring into their compositions as many features of Cage's piece as they can: the variety of rhythmic patterns, the fading in and out of different elements of the music, the use of a range of timbres and so on. Above all, ask them to make sure that they *listen* to the rest of their group at all times.

Give the children about 15 minutes to work on their compositions, then bring the class back together for each group to perform to the others. Record each one if possible, and finish the session by playing 'Second Construction' again and asking the children to compare it with their own (see 'Moving forward').

Suggestion(s) for extension

Children who have shown particular sensitivity in this activity can be asked to compose a rhythmic piece incorporating *silences* as well as sounds. This will require them to listen even more carefully to each other to ensure that they create a silence, and to plan carefully so that they know where they will occur in the piece.

Suggestion(s) for support

Some children will find it hard to make sense of the unconventional style of John Cage's music, particularly if they have not heard anything like it before. The more times they listen to it, the easier they will find it to understand. It will help if you ask them to listen out for certain sounds or instruments, for example the snare drum or the sheet metal, and to raise a hand each time this sound appears.

Assessment opportunities

You can use this activity to monitor children's awareness of musical style, as well as their ability to reproduce a particular style in their own compositions and listen carefully to music.

Display ideas

The idea of a 'Sound Cage' can be used as the basis of a display, with children's representations of their own rhythms and sounds contained within the cage. You could make the recordings of the Cage piece and the children's own compositions available for listening to next to the display. This work could also be linked to an art project investigating the modern art styles of the 1930s and 1940s. For example, reproductions of the work of Dali, Matisse or Picasso could be displayed alongside the 'Sound Cage', with children's descriptions of the ways in which both visual artists and composers of the time were experimenting with unconventional ideas and effects.

Opportunities for IT

The children could program a range of rhythmic patterns into a keyboard or computer, then create a composition by selecting the rhythms in a chosen order. They could use a drawing package to create their own 'Sound Cage' sheets, using the edit facility to try out different ideas.

Moving forward

The children could follow up these two sessions by comparing their own compositions with the John Cage piece, using sheet 133. You might also like them to evaluate their compositions or performances using either sheet 151 or sheet 152. The children could appraise the Cage piece in a different way by drawing a journey line of it (see page 44). They could also move on to listening to the works of other contemporary composers, such as Philip Glass, Arvo Pärt or Harrison Birtwhistle and try to recreate the particular styles of these composers.

World Music

World music is the term used to describe non-Western music, from both the folk and classical traditions. It covers such a wide variety of styles and instruments that no one could be an expert on the whole range. Some of this music may seem so unfamiliar that you find it hard to make sense of it. However, there is really no difference between the way you use world music in the classroom and the way you would use any other music: through listening, exploring, thinking and experimenting. In this chapter only a glimpse can be given of the vast range of music you might work with, but this should give you a starting-point from which you can explore further. Music in this chapter includes a Tunisian pop song, traditional Northumbrian pipe music, Chinese folk music, West African rhythms and classical music of Thailand and India. In each case, enough information is given about the music for you and your pupils to begin to understand and work with it. You could also use activities from the *Listening* chapter to explore ways of responding to music from different parts of the world.

Examples of all these types of music are included on the cassette that can be purchased with this book, but recordings of world music are also readily available in high street music stores. You may prefer to select your own styles and recordings and adapt the activities accordingly. (The sleeve notes accompanying these recordings can be extremely informative.) It is a good idea to support your lessons with additional resources (artefacts, pictures or videos) to help set the music in context.

ZEIN'S TUNE

To introduce some of the main features of Arabic music.

♪♪ *Whole class.*

🕐 *45 minutes.*

♫ *Easy.*

Previous skills/knowledge needed

Any activity that helps children to develop their vocabulary for talking about music would be useful, for example the vocabulary or music review sheets for the activity 'Talking about music' on page 40.

Key background information

Arabic music refers to a long and wide-ranging tradition of music. It is not the country of Arabia that is referred to, rather the Arab cultures. Middle-Eastern music might be a better description. This area stretches from North Africa, eastwards to Uzbekistan in the Russian Union.

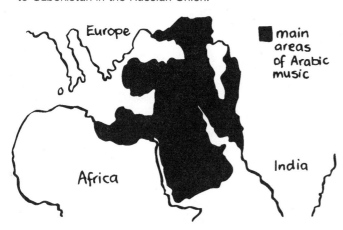

Arabic music uses *modal* scales, which gives it its distinctive quality. A modal scale is an arrangement of notes that have larger and smaller intervals between each note. In the diatonic scale, common in Western music, the intervals are more even. The modal style is highlighted by singing or playing the melody line. Flourishes and slides with the voice give a highly distinctive way of singing that is associated with the 'Arabic' style. It is similar to some Indian classical singing or melody playing.

The piece of music used in this activity is a Tunisian pop song entitled 'Your Love is Wisdom', sung in Arabic, composed in a folk style by a well-known contemporary Tunisian musician: Zein Safi (Zein is pronounced 'zeen'). He uses keyboard and drum kit alongside the lute and traditional goblet-shaped drum called a dabourka. The lute or 'el oud' was brought over to Great Britain from North Africa by the returning Crusaders and became a favourite instrument of the Tudor period.

The dabourka is played with fingertips. The high pitch sound that results from the very tight skin on the drum is a distinctive feature of Arabic music. Rhythm also plays a prominent part in this style of music with drumming patterns being meticulously memorised using a verbal form of explanation. Many different notes can be achieved on the instrument, for example, 'Ta, ticka, ticka ta, Ta ticka, ticka ta.' The 'Ta' indicates a low note made by striking the middle of the drum skin, whereas the 'Ticka' is a high sound made by striking the skin near the side of the drum. A song may often have nothing but a drum accompaniment.

Vocabulary

Modal, lute, el oud, darbourka, Arabic.

Preparation

Listen to 'Your Love is Wisdom' available on the cassette (that can be purchased to accompany this book), so that you are aware of the combination of instruments and some of the rhythms used. If you are not using the music from the cassette, choose a piece of Arabic music that shows the influence of Western pop, either through use of a keyboard, amplified drum kit or something similar. The music you choose should have a distinctive melody line, either sung or played, that uses scales decorated by flourishes and turns of the voice. You also need to choose a piece of modern pop music that has a melody, accompaniment and drum beat. Try out a few of the practice drumming rhythms on photocopiable sheet 141. To make the high 'Ticka' tap on the table with your fingertips (not nails), to play the low 'Ta' use the second and third finger on the same hand. Find a map that shows North Africa, the Middle East and Europe.

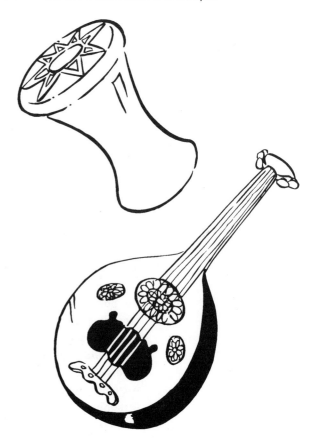

Resources needed

Recording of 'Your Love is Wisdom' composed by Zein Safi and Ben Hadj (Phonie), or other recording of Arabic music, a piece of Western pop/modern music, cassette player, copy of photocopiable sheet 133 for each child, copy of photocopiable sheet 141 for yourself, pencils, map (see 'Preparation'), A3 sheet of paper pinned to the wall or use of a white board, felt-tipped pens.

What to do

Tell the children that they are going to be listening to music from North Africa. Show them the map and point out the position of the Mediterranean Sea. Make reference to the trading that has happened between European and North African countries since before the time of the Roman Empire. Explain how music is influenced by other cultures all the time.

Before they listen to any music, tell the children they are going to practise playing a drumming rhythm that might go with the music. Show them the use of 'Ta' and 'Ticka' to make low and high sounds and play the first rhythm from photocopiable sheet 141. Go through the first rhythm with the class using the method of 'copy and echo' (see the activity on page 19 for an example of this) where they repeat back to you what you have played. Teach them as many of the rhythms on the sheet as they need to make them confident with this method of playing.

Play Zein's tune for two minutes. When it has finished ask the children to tell you one thing that sounds familiar to them. Choose four or five children to write down their answers on the A3 sheet of paper. Tell them that you are going to play the music again and this time you want them to listen for things that sound different and unfamiliar. After three minutes stop the tape and hear what they have to say. You may get comments such as: 'The singing is funny' or 'The words sound odd'. Use the comments that they make as the prompt for questions. Ask them things such as: 'Why do the words sound odd?'; 'Tell me more about the funny singing'; 'Is it different from or the same as how you sing?'; 'In what way is it different?' The purpose of these sort of questions is to highlight the fact that there is a particular style involved in the singing which is very much a part of Arabic music.

Say that you are going to play the music again and this time you want the children to listen out for the percussion section and particularly the drum. As they hear the rhythm, let them quietly join in by tapping with three fingers in the way they practised earlier.

Now play them the Western pop/modern music and ask them to listen for things that sound familiar and perhaps similar to Zein's tune, and things that sound totally different. Hand out the photocopiable sheet 133 and play Zein's tune one more time before you ask them to fill it in.

Now tell the children that they are going to listen to Arabic music and that you want them to listen carefully for sounds that are familiar (instruments or style of playing). Make it clear that everyone will be familiar with different sorts of music and that there is no right or wrong answer.

Suggestion(s) for extension

If the children have found this activity easy, ask them to listen a few more times to hear how the more detailed percussion rhythms go and then join in with those. Ask them to make up their own 'Ta, ticka' pattern to fit the music.

Suggestion(s) for support

If the children are finding the activity hard, ask them to keep a simple beat with a rhythm as they listen. Support their 'Ta, Ticka' rhythms by saying the words with them while they tap them out. You could also give them their own copy of sheet 141 to help them follow the rhythm, but this is not, ideally, how they are supposed to learn.

Assessment opportunities

Use this activity to assess the children's awareness of the main characteristics of different styles of music.

Opportunities for IT

The children could use a CD-ROM to research more information about Arabic music and instruments.

Display ideas

Display the children's comparisons sheets alongside a simple explanation of how to learn the drumming rhythms.

Reference to photocopiable sheets

Sheet 133 invites the children to compare the two pieces of music. Sheet 141 sets out a few drum rhythms written using the 'Ta, ticka' idea, and provides space for you to invent your own.

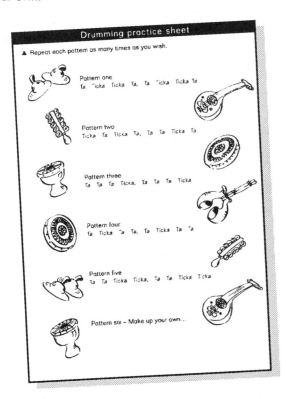

Moving forward

If you want to become more familiar with Tunisian music there are many different ways of listening which are described in the *Listening* chapter. 'Sleeping angels' in this chapter involves listening to and playing in the style of a type of music.

FOLK PATTERNS

To introduce Western European folk music and develop awareness of its structure through the use of movement.

†† *Whole class, then groups of four.*

🕐 *45 minutes.*

♫ *Easy.*

Previous skills/knowledge needed

If the children have had some previous experience of folk dancing, this will help them to devise their own dance steps. However, this is not essential.

Key background information

Throughout the world, three of the most important purposes of folk music are entertainment, storytelling and dance. It is music designed to captivate and involve its listeners. The style of folk music differs from one country to another, and even from one area to another, but there are also strong similarities. One particular characteristic of almost all the folk music of the British Isles, for example, is the type of structure (sometimes known as A – B – A – B) in which a first tune is followed by a second one, then the first is repeated, followed by the second one again. This simple structure is explored in this activity, and used as the basis for the invention of dances. In turn, creating the dances will give children an insight into the structure of the music, and the rhythmic movements of their dance steps will help them to feel its rhythm. Music for dance has been focused on, rather than music for storytelling, to encourage the children to listen to music rather than words. A traditional tune played by Kathryn Tickell on the Northumbrian pipes has been used (available on the cassette), but you could use any folk tune which moves fast enough for people to dance to, and which has two alternating tunes following an A – B – A – B structure.

Vocabulary

Folk, pattern, structure.

Preparation

Listen to 'Mary the Maid', or your own choice of music, and note for yourself when the music changes from Tune A to Tune B and back again. Practise clapping 16 slow beats for each section of the music. You will probably be able to hear that each tune is played twice before the next one comes in, so that the overall structure of the music is really A A B B A A B B. You might like to start this activity off in the classroom, but move into the school hall for the children to make up their dances.

Resources needed

Recording of 'Mary the Maid' by Kathryn Tickell (Black Crow Records), or your own choice of music, cassette player.

What to do

Play the recording of 'Mary the Maid' to the children, asking them to listen carefully. Discuss the music with them briefly: it is a traditional tune played on the Northumbrian pipes, a smaller cousin of the Scottish bagpipes. Ask the children to listen again, this time focusing on what happens to the tune. Play the music up to the point where the tune changes (after a slow count of 16) then stop the recording just after the tune has changed. Ask the children whether this is the same tune – they will almost certainly answer no! Carry on listening, and again stop the recording where the first tune returns. Ask the children about this tune – do they recognise it as the one they heard at the beginning? Carry on again until the third and final change – do the children recognise this as the second tune they heard? Talk about the structure of the piece with them, clarifying the A – B – A – B pattern. Listen to the music again, this time asking the children to clap in time with it and count the number of claps in each section. You will find that there are 16 claps before the tune changes. Ask the children to remember this, as it will be important for their next task.

Now take the children into the school hall, or a similar large space. Explain that you would like them to make up their own folk dances to go with the music they have just heard, working in groups of four. Tell them that their dances must have the same structure as the music, so that the two fit together. Their dances, therefore, will be divided into four sections, and they will need to count to 16 for each section, before changing to a new move to keep in line with each change in the tune.

Suggest that each group starts in a circle. For the first section they could take steps into the centre and back (four forward, four backwards and repeat), or join hands and circle round for a count of 16, or join hands in the centre to form a star, taking eight clockwise and eight anti-clockwise steps. Ask them to make suggestions and try out some ideas, putting them together into a dance of their own. Play the music several times while they are working so that they can practise fitting their dances into it. Remind the children that their movements must change each time the music changes. Give them plenty of opportunity to practise their dances all the way through before asking them to perform them in front of the rest of the class.

Finish the lesson by asking each group to demonstrate their dance to the others, and inviting the other children to comment, thinking particularly about the way their movements fit in with the music.

Suggestion(s) for extension

Children who have worked well with this activity, showing an understanding of the structure of the music, can try composing their own simple dance tunes, based on the same principle of four sections, each divided into a count of 16.

Suggestion(s) for support

Some children will find it hard to feel the pulse of the music and may be unable to move in time or plan a series of dance

movements to go with it. It is a good idea to pair these children with those who are responding more confidently to the music. It is also essential to give them as much opportunity to practise as possible – most of their difficulties may simply be due to a lack of experience.

Assessment opportunities

This activity allows you to assess children's awareness of a particular style of music, and their ability to respond to music with movement.

Opportunities for IT

The children could use a word processor to write the instructions for their dance so that someone else could perform it. They might even extend the instructions by using a drawing package to make a visual representation of the dance, for example:

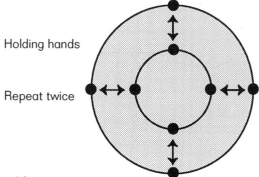

Display ideas

Photographs (or videos) of the children performing their dances can be displayed alongside an explanation of the activity. You could also have the recorded music available nearby so that the children can listen to it and remind themselves of their dances.

Moving forward

You can explore dance further through the activity 'Waltzing Victorians' on page 65, or you could use folk music from any part of the world as a focus for the activities in the *Listening* chapter.

Previous skills/knowledge needed

Children need to have experience of playing a xylophone, see 'Introducing scales' on page 23.

Key background information

China is a huge and diverse country and its music reflects this diversity. Defining a single style of genuine Chinese music would be impossible, as each *region* has its own type of traditional instruments and as many types of folk and classical music as in the West. However, it is possible to create a flavour of traditional Chinese music by using *fourths* on the xylophone. The music provided on the cassette that accompanies the book uses the Chinese pipes or plucked lute. Fourths refers to playing two notes together that are a particular distance apart. This can be best illustrated by looking on a xylophone or keyboard. (See diagram below.)

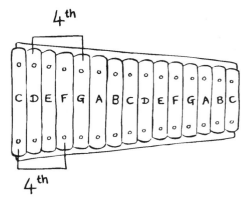

The distance between two notes is called an *interval*. If the lower note changes then the upper note will alter in a similar way, so that the two notes played always remain the same distance apart.

Vocabulary

Interval, fourths.

Preparation

If you want to increase your confidence, practise playing fourths up and down a xylophone in single steps. Have ready all the instruments listed below. Any pictures you have of traditional Chinese folk instruments would be useful for comparisons, but are not essential.

Listen to 'Lanterns and Moon Competing in Brilliance' on the cassette. The 'Lanterns' in the title refers to the Lantern Festival held at Chinese New Year. This particular music uses many short repeated phrases and additional rhythms. Alternatively, choose your own piece of Chinese music.

Resources needed

Extract of traditional Chinese music or 'Lanterns and Moon Competing in Brilliance' (from *Chinese Music for the Pipa* [Nimbus]). For each group you will need: a xylophone and four beaters (two would suffice); a quiet drum and/or claves; set of temple bells (jingle bells would be fine); a pair of chime bars that sound a fourth apart (C & F, D & G, E & A); a cymbal if you have one.

they wish to go up the xylophone before they come back down the scale in their fourths. (It is easier to go up only four notes before coming down.) Give out the rest of the instruments and, still working as a whole class, have another practice of the drums and claves accompanying the xylophones. This time suggest that after the players have gone up and down the scale, all the chime bars and temple bells will play a big 'clash'. Doing this introduces the idea of structure to the piece which the children can follow up and develop themselves.

Now talk to them about the different combinations in

What to do

Introduce the idea of working with Chinese sounds by playing an extract of Chinese folk music and showing the children the pictures of instruments. Ask them if they recognise any instruments or if they can imagine the sounds that might be made by them. Explain that they are going to create a composition of something that represents a tiny part of Chinese music. Demonstrate the use of a fourth on the xylophone. Show the children how the interval works by counting out the distance that it covers. Remember to point out that counting an interval in music is different from counting on in mathematics, as the note you start on counts as one! Get two children to demonstrate playing consecutive fourths. It is easier and sounds more effective if you play four quick beats on each note before moving on to the next note. Your playing might be something like this:

```
CCCC   DDDD   EEEE   DDDD   CCCC   DDDD   EEE
FFFF   GGGG   AAAA   GGGG   FFAA   GGGG   AA
```

Give out a xylophone, beaters and drums to each group. As a whole class practise playing the fourths together. Ask all the xylophone players to play their fourths, and the drums and claves to join in by tapping out a quiet rhythm – either a slow one to every four of the xylophone, or a quick light tap at the same pace as the xylophone.

When the children are accustomed to the rhythm, ask the xylophones to play up and down the instruments in fourths. Remind them that they will have to decide how far

which they could play their instruments, for example: the xylophone and drum could be followed by a pause, before the claves bring the beat back in and further playing on the xylophones could be interrupted by a loud clash on cymbals and bells. Give the children five minutes to practise. As all the groups will be practising at the same time, this will be very loud, but you will find that all the children are concentrating and trying out many productive ideas with each other.

Stop the practice after about four minutes and remind the class of the task as well as picking out examples of children who are playing fourths well, or working well as a group. As the children will not be able to hear what they are playing in detail, it is important to give them time to show their work to each other. For the grand finale, ask each group to play what they have done. When each group is playing, emphasise the importance of the role of the rest of the class as audience. If you can convey to the children a feeling of concentration, which shows that the work is being taken seriously, then the results will be of a far greater standard.

Suggestion(s) for extension

If some children adapt to the fourths with ease, ask them to make up a simple tune in fourths that they can add into their compositions in whatever way they choose.

Suggestion(s) for support

If the children find the activity difficult, stipulate a simple arrangement of fourths for them to play and ask them to add in the percussion accompaniment.

AFRICAN POLYRHYTHMS

To develop awareness of African rhythms and give experience of complex rhythms.

♯♯ *Whole class.*

🕐 *Two 30-minute sessions.*

♫ *Medium.*

Previous skills/knowledge needed

For this activity the children need to be able to keep a beat and play a rhythm. 'Copy and echo' and 'Controlling tempo' on pages 19 and 21 give experience of these skills. The activity 'Multibeat' in *Using voices and bodies* in the Key Stage 1 book introduces polyrhythms by using voices and simple words.

Key background information

Many forms of music use rhythms which are more complicated than the 1, 2, 3, 4 beat that we can often pick out in Western classical music. Rhythms that span over 5, 7 or 9 beats are common in much African, Asian and Latin American music. In this activity, African music and rhythms are used. It is important to remember when talking about Africa or its music, that it is a huge continent with many different styles. In this activity a piece called 'Salikaro' is listened to with rhythms which are simple when played by themselves. When these rhythms are played together they form an exciting complex rhythmic sequence. The best way to experience the feel of these complicated rhythms is to play them. *Polyrhythms* (or cross rhythms) is the term used to describe many rhythms played at one time.

Assessment opportunities

You will be able to assess the children's ability to imitate the characteristic feature of a particular style of music.

Opportunities for IT

The children could use software such as *Music Explorer* or *Music Box* to set up their own tunes using fourths. These could be recorded by the computer and saved as a file so that they can be played back later on. Children might also like to experiment with the stereotypical Chinese-style music that forms part of the *Compose* (BBC/Nimbus) or *Compose World* software (PC and Acorn RISCOS).

Display ideas

Take photographs of the children composing and performing the music. Mount these alongside pictures of traditional Chinese folk instruments and ask the children to write about the similarities and differences of the instruments and music.

Moving forward

If you wish to explore composing with different styles of music, 'Sleeping angels' and 'Recreating a raga' in this chapter would both be suitable activities. If you wish to explore Chinese music further, the *Listening* chapter has many activities that will enable you to do this. Skills in xylophone playing are explored further in 'Jumped up Mozart' on page 59.

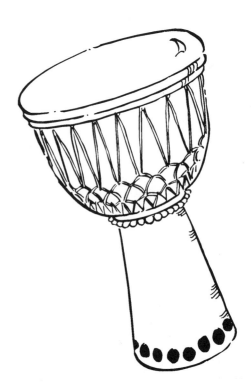

Vocabulary
Polyrhythms, cross rhythms.

Preparation
If you do not wish to use 'Salikaro' that is available on the cassette, then collect any recording of African drumming, as it is likely to include polyrhythms. Prepare the recording and listen to the music in advance.

Resources needed
A recording of 'Salikaro' by Paul Horn (Celestial Harmonies), or other recording of African drumming, cassette player.

For session two you will need a selection of untuned instruments.

What to do
Session one
Introduce the idea of African music to the children and explain that they are going to be playing African rhythms. Ask them to join you in lightly clapping a continuous steady pulse that accentuates the first of every four beats: 1 2 3 4 1 2 3 4 1 2 3 4 1 2 3 4. When they are happy with this, ask them to clap only on the first of every four beats, counting the other beats silently in their heads.

Tell them you are going to introduce counting in threes. Do this in exactly the same way as you introduced counting in fours, but only accentuate the first of every three beats, not four: 1 2 3 1 2 3 1 2 3 1 2 3.

> **Four-beat rhythm:**
> 1 2 3 4 1 2 3 4 1 2 3 4 1 2 3 4
> **Three-beat rhythm:**
> 1 2 3 1 2 3 1 2 3 1 2 3 1 2 3 1

When the class is confident with this, play the following '3/4' game. Ask all the class to clap the four-beat rhythm. Do this six or seven times, then without losing the steady pulse, shout 'change' – straightaway the children change to clapping the three-beat rhythm. After six or seven times of the three-beat rhythm shout 'change' again and the children have to clap the four-beat rhythm. Try to shout 'change' on the first beat, or 1, of the counting as this avoids confusion.

When you feel they have grasped what to do, ask half the class to clap the four-beat rhythm and the other half the three-beat rhythm. Start the groups off together so that they have their very first clap at the same time. Getting everyone to start together can be difficult, so rather than 1, 2, 3 or 1, 2, 3, 4, use a made up set of words which will indicate the speed of the pulse that everyone will be clapping to. You could use a nonsense phrase such as 'apple, plum, tomato'. To start with, the class will find this difficult, but with concentration they will be able follow their own pattern while maintaining a steady common pulse. It will help them if they watch other people in their own rhythm group.

At the end of the session, play them 'Salikaro' and discuss what they have heard. Can they hear similarities to what they have been doing? Is the recorded music different?

Session two

Revise the work covered in the previous session, paying particular attention to the need to concentrate when playing rhythms. When the class is able to clap in threes and fours together, you can introduce fives, sevens, and elevens. However, it may take several weeks for them to clap all these combinations at the same time.

They could practise by using instruments, to play the '1' of each rhythm. As a variation on this, ask the children to use a sound effect for the '1' instead of a clap or an instrument. These sound effects could be linked to a topic, for instance those related to a Victorian street scene, a tropical rain forest, a farmyard or factory.

When you use instruments or sound effects to replace each clap, ask the children to notice the different 'texture' that it creates. Both this and the sound-effects variation highlight the feeling of rhythms continuously crossing each other to create an intricate sound pattern, as well as providing a good opportunity to explore 'timbre' (type of sound) and 'texture' (how the sound is built up in the music).

Suggestion(s) for extension

If the children find this activity easy, ask a small group or individual to play each rhythm. Encourage them to experiment with longer rhythms – a 13 or 17 – or ask the children to predict when their first-beat clap will coincide and decide on a particular sound to use for this.

Suggestion(s) for support

If the children find the activity hard, go back to clapping the four-beat rhythm and then build up to using two rhythms.

Alternatively, as a class record the four-beat rhythm and clap the three-beat rhythm with the recording playing. If a particular child is finding the rhythms difficult, stand him or her next to someone who is confident.

Assessment opportunities

Use this activity to assess the children's awareness of the characteristics of different styles of music and their ability to play complex rhythms.

Opportunities for IT

The children could use the 'Beat Box' part of the *Music Box* computer software to build up their own polyrhythms.

Using computer graphics from a drawing package or word processor, copy out the pattern of the rhythm. Find a way, using different fonts, symbols and sizes, to emphasise the places where the first beats of different patterns coincide with each other.

Display ideas

Ask the children to write out the rhythms on paper showing where the first beat of the different rhythms coincide. By doing this, the mathematics of the activity will be highlighted. This could also be done using a computer (see above).

Moving forward

The rhythmic awareness developed in this activity would be particularly useful for the activity 'Performance poetry' on page 34 which makes rhythmic use of words for composing. This activity leads well into 'Sound cage' on page 68, which explores unconventional rhythm combinations.

SLEEPING ANGELS

To develop awareness of the music of South-East Asia
and to use a similar style in composition.

†† *Whole class, then groups of five or six.*

🕐 *45 minutes.*

♫ *Medium.*

Previous skills/knowledge needed

The children will need to have some familiarity with tuned percussion instruments such as xylophones, metallophones or chime bars. 'Introducing scales' on page 23 would provide useful experience here. If the children have already had some experience of listening to and describing non-Western music (for example, through working with 'Zein's tune', 'Chinese whispers' or 'African polyrhythms' in this chapter or through using non-Western music with any of the activities in the *Listening* chapter) it will help them to listen carefully to the music used here.

Key background information

This activity uses the classical music of Thailand as a stimulus: a style of music which draws partly on the traditions of China and India, but which has most in common with the Gamelan music of Java and Bali (a Gamelan is a collection of gongs, xylophones and drums) and the similar musical styles of Myanmar and Cambodia. This style of music was intended for court entertainment (this particular example originates from the mid-nineteenth century) but was often taken from earlier folk versions. The example on the cassette is entitled 'The Sleeping Angel', and uses sequences of descending notes on xylophones and flute to suggest an angel lying down to rest. The activity encourages the children to conjure up a similar musical image using xylophones, metallophones and chime bars. An even more authentic effect can be gained by adding finger cymbals, wooden clappers and low-pitched drums. If any of the children in your class play recorders, they can use these to represent the Thai flute. The angel referred to in the title of the piece is a

figure from Hindu mythology who protected Rama and his brother Lakshman from the demon Ravana. The importance of Hindu mythology in the largely Buddhist culture of Thailand reflects the way that religions, like music, grow and develop from a range of influences.

If you do not want to use the example on the cassette, you can obtain suitable recordings from music shops; this activity would work equally well with music from Java, Bali, Myanmar, Cambodia or Thailand.

Vocabulary

Thailand, timbre, style, descending, pattern, sequence, pentatonic scale (see 'Preparation').

Preparation

Listen to the recording of 'The Sleeping Angel' (or your own choice of music). Play it several times so that you become familiar with it. Collect together any supporting resource materials you might have which would help to set the music in context (for example, photographs or videos, particularly any which show music, art or dance of the country – the Siamese-style performance of 'Uncle Tom's Cabin' in the film *The King and I*, gives a surprisingly accurate impression of music and dance from this part of the world). Prepare the xylophones, metallophones and chime bars by replacing all the Bs with B flats and removing all notes except F G B flat C and D. This sequence of notes forms a *pentatonic* scale, which is characteristic of the music of South-East Asia. (If you do not have B flats, use F, G, A, C and D.) Set the instruments out so that they are within easy reach of you and the children. Provide enough instruments for everyone to play at once, including yourself; larger instruments such as xylophones can be shared between two players. If you want the children to notate their compositions, they will need paper and pencils. However, it is perfectly acceptable for them to compose and play their pieces without writing anything down.

Resources needed

Recording of 'The Sleeping Angel' (from *The Sleeping Angel: Thai Classical Music* [Nimbus]), or your own choice of music, cassette player, supporting resource materials, prepared xylophones, metallophones and chime bars, blank cassette, paper and pencils. Optional: low-pitched drums, finger cymbals and wooden clappers, recorders or penny whistles.

What to do

Without giving out any instruments, play the recording of 'The Sleeping Angel' twice to the class. Ask the children to describe what they can hear: What sort of instruments are being used? Is the music loud or quiet, slow or fast, aggressive or gentle? Explain the background to the music (see 'Key background information') and show them any supporting resource materials you have.

Play the music again, and while they are listening, ask the children to select instruments which make similar sounds to those in the recording and to join in while it is playing. They might choose to play a sequence of notes on xylophones, metallophones or chime bars, or they might echo the percussion part using drums, finger cymbals or clappers. (These are quite hard to hear in the recording at first, but the children may gradually become aware of them playing throughout the piece.) Once all the children have joined in, fade out the recorded music and ask the children to keep

going. It will help if you play too, so that you are all part of one large ensemble. Keep playing together for a minute or two, so that you can hear yourselves as a group. Finish with a single stroke on a low note of a xylophone or metallophone to bring your performance to an end.

Discuss the music with the class. Did what you were playing sound like the music you heard in the recording? If so, why? If not, why not? Is there something missing that could be added to make a more authentic sound? Suggest any instruments that have not yet been used, and ask the children with drums to make their pattern follow the one in the recording. Point out to those playing tuned instruments that the music in the recording uses sequences of descending notes to create the image of the angel lying down to sleep, and suggest that they try doing the same. There is a sequence repeated three times towards the end of the extract which uses roughly these notes (it is difficult to achieve the exact equivalent using Western instruments):

B♭	D	C	B♭	B♭	C	B♭
D	C	B♭	G	G		
C	B♭	G	F	F		
B♭	G	F	D	D		

You could write this sequence of notes on the board or a large sheet of paper and ask the children to try playing it alongside the recording. Alternatively, suggest that they use the notes F, G, B flat, C and D in a combination of their choice. (These will be the only notes available on the xylophones and so on, but children playing recorders will need to select these notes themselves.)

Give the children some time to work on the new ideas you and they have suggested, then practise the piece together, incorporating any new features. When they are ready, play along with the recording again, then fade it out and continue to play and finish as before with a single low note. Once the children are satisfied that they are making an authentic sound as a whole class, split the class into groups of five or six, each with a combination of tuned and untuned instruments from the selection you have been using. Ask each group to compose their own piece of music, keeping as closely as they can to the sound and style of the music in the recording. They might like to think of a new title and compose a piece that reflects it. (If you have been studying Hindu mythology with the class, you could suggest they choose another event from the Ramayana.) If you want the children to notate their compositions, give out pencils and paper. Their notation might look something like this:

cymbals	*			*		
xylophones	F	G	B♭ G	B♭	C	B♭
recorders	F		F		F		F
drums	X		x x	X	x	x

cymbals	*			*		
xylophones	C	D	C B♭	G		G
recorders	G		G		G		G
drums	X		x x	X	x	x

cymbals	*			*		
xylophones	G	B♭ G	F	D	F	D
recorders	G		G		G		G
drums	X		x x	X	x	x

cymbals	*			*		
xylophones	F	D	C	D	C		C
recorders	F		F		F		F
drums	X		x x	X	x	x

Give the groups about 20 minutes to work on their compositions, then bring the whole class back together, and ask each group to play their piece to the others. After they have all played their compositions once, ask the groups to play one after the other to create a continuous piece. Record these performances if possible so the children can hear the effect (you might like to refine them further in a future session).

Conclude the lesson with a grand performance: start by playing along with the recording as at the beginning of the session, continue with the group compositions played one

after another, then finish with a whole-class improvisation in the same style, ending at a signal from you (or from a child chosen to conduct) with a single low note, or fading out one instrument at a time to finish with a single note.

Suggestion(s) for extension

The ensemble in the recording uses a glass xylophone (called a 'renat kaeo'). Children who have shown an ability to recreate the pattern of notes used in 'Sleeping Angel' can try to create a similar sequence using bottles or glasses filled with different levels of water, tapping them with metal triangle or rubber xylophone beaters to make their own 'renat kaeo'. An advantage of using this rather than a Western xylophone is that the children can play 'between' the notes of the Western scale, creating a more authentic 'South-East Asian sound'.

Suggestion(s) for support

Some children may find it hard to hear the different instrument sounds within the recorded music. Tell them to listen for specific sounds or instruments and allow them to listen to the music repeatedly so that they become increasingly familiar with it.

Assessment opportunities

This activity provides opportunities to monitor children's awareness of different musical styles and their ability to use a specific style in composition. You will also be able to note their ability to work collaboratively on a composition task, to prepare and give a performance, and to keep in time with each other.

World Music

Opportunities for IT

The children could use a music composition package such as *Music Explorer* or *Music Box* to create their own computer-generated Thai-style music. Using a pentatonic scale such as the one suggested in this activity (F, G, B flat, C, D) will help to give the music an authentic flavour.

The children could also use a CD-ROM encyclopaedia or specialist music CD-ROM such as Microsoft's *Musical Instruments* to research other information about South-East Asian music. The children could go on to create a multi-media presentation using authoring software to represent the information they have discovered along with recorded versions of their own music as a background. The presentation could contain text and pictures taken from CD-ROMs, drawn using an art package or scanned from their own line drawings or photographs.

Display ideas

Displays could show photographs of Thai musicians, dancers and art alongside descriptions of the Thai music you have used and the children's own compositions. This presents a good opportunity to demonstrate the way in which different art-forms are all used for a common purpose.

Moving forward

The principle behind this activity can be applied to different types of music, for example, it works very well with Shona music from Zimbabwe, where voices, xylophones and rattles can be used to create Shona-type compositions. The focus here on the sounds and structure within a particular style leads well into 'Recreating a Raga' in this chapter, while the children could apply the skills they have developed here to any of the activities in the *Composing* chapter. The music of South-East Asia had a strong influence on the work of John Cage, whose music is used as a stimulus for 'Sound cage' on page 68.

 **RECREATING A RAGA**

To familiarise children with the sound and structure of Indian ragas.

†† *Whole class, working in groups of three.*
🕐 *60 minutes, or two 30-minute sessions.*
♫ *Advanced.*

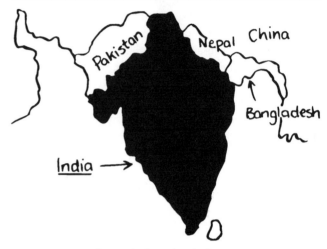

Previous skills/knowledge needed

The children will need to have gained some familiarity with non-Western music (by doing some of the activities in this chapter, or by using world music for some activities in the *Listening* chapter). 'Sleeping angels' in this chapter links particularly well with this activity, as it also focuses on reproducing the characteristic sound of a certain type of music. It will help if the children are familiar with the pattern tracking sheet 142 (see 'Pattern tracking' on page 96 if you have not used this before), but this is not essential. They will also need to be fairly confident in using tuned and untuned instruments and to have some awareness of informal notation – the use of patterns and symbols to represent sounds. 'Graphic notation – instant composition' on page 108 provides useful background experience.

Key background information

To those who are not accustomed to it, Indian music may seem like one long drone with no apparent structure. However, all Indian music is actually highly structured, with each type having its own characteristic sounds and patterns. The type investigated in this activity is the *raga*, a form of music from the Indian classical tradition with its own complex history, mythology and theory. A raga is a sequence of five to seven notes, from which a melodic pattern is created. ('Raga' is actually a Sanskrit word meaning 'that which pleases'.) Each raga is associated with a certain mood and a certain time of day. The one used on the cassette is 'Raga Bhimpalasi', which is associated with the dreamy moods induced by the sultry heat of the Indian afternoon.

Although it is difficult to represent the notes of a raga accurately on Western instruments, because Indian music

uses *microtones* (gaps between notes which are far smaller than those of Western music), a sequence of notes similar to that used in this raga can be obtained by playing the white notes of a keyboard, starting from D. (In Western music this sequence is known as the Dorian mode, or D-mode. It is common in old English tunes such as 'Greensleeves' and 'Scarborough Fair'.)

In the extract used on the cassette, you will hear a *rising* sequence (played on the bamboo flute) performed with a variety of different embellishments; followed each time by a *falling* sequence. (The difference between the upward and downward sequences gives each raga its characteristic sound.) You could play these two sequences on a keyboard or xylophone using the following notes (this follows the pattern used in the recording, but at a different pitch):

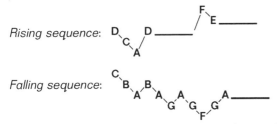

The lines represent long notes, while the placing of notes at different heights shows the pattern of the sequence.

This pattern could also be represented very simply by two lines like this:

Rising sequences:

Falling sequences:

The children will use patterns of this sort to represent the raga in this activity (see 'What to do').

If you prefer to use your own choice of raga, you will find recordings are readily available in high street music stores. Whichever raga you choose, you will hear the same structure – a free-flowing introduction (this can last for ten minutes or more), followed by a whole host of variations with a rhythmic accompaniment (usually played on a drum called a *tabla*) and an underlying drone (a continuous background note or notes often played, as in this example, on a multi-stringed instrument called a *tanpura* or *tambura*).

Vocabulary

Raga, Bhimpalasi, microtones, tanpura, tabla, drone, melody, rhythm, graphic score.

Preparation

Check that you have a suitable range of instruments for the activity (see 'Resources needed'). Listen to the recording of 'Raga Bhimpalasi' (or your own choice of raga) and use a copy of the pattern tracking sheet 142 to try and analyse the music as you listen. Your analysis will need to show the *drone*, the *melody* (tune) and the *rhythm*. Use three different colours to represent these elements of the music, drawing whatever patterns or symbols you like on to the sheet, to show what you hear. Try putting the first sequence (flute and tanpura only) in the first section of the chart, then indicating how many times this is repeated with the drumming accompaniment in the second section. Next indicate the two slower versions of the same sequence in the third section, followed by the longer, lower notes in the fourth section, leading into the final long note in the fifth section. Your analysis does not have to be perfect, you are simply having a go at what the children will be doing and making your own version to discuss with them later.

Make one enlarged (A3) copy of the pattern tracking sheet 142 for each group. If you would like the children to use sheets 133 and 135, make copies for each group.

Resources needed

Cassette player, blank cassette, recording of 'Raga Bhimpalasi' performed by Hariprasad Chaurasia and Fazal Qureshi (Nimbus), or your own choice of raga, a range of instruments (xylophones, keyboards, recorders, penny whistles, violins, guitars, drums) enough for each group to have a mixture of tuned and untuned instruments, one copy of the pattern tracking sheet 142 for each group plus your own completed sheet (see 'Preparation'), one copy of sheets 133 and 135 for each group (optional), white board or flip chart, marker pens, three different-coloured pens or pencils.

What to do

Sit the children in groups of three and play them the recording of 'Raga Bhimpalasi'. Ask them to listen carefully, noticing how the music starts, how it continues and what kinds of instruments are used. Discuss what they have heard, and tell them what you know about ragas (see 'Key background information').

Now give each group a copy of photocopiable page 142 and a set of three coloured pens or pencils; then play the recording again. This time, tell the members of each group that they are going to use the sheet to represent what they hear, using different colours for the drone, the melody and the rhythm. They will need to listen to the music several times to do this. Play it through once, discussing how the different parts might be represented, then play just the first part, where the sequence is played a total of five times. Ask whether they can hear a difference between the first time and the next four: the children may notice that the drum only comes in after the first sequence. Guide them through filling in their sheets (see 'Preparation'). Play the recording as many times as necessary for them to fill them in.

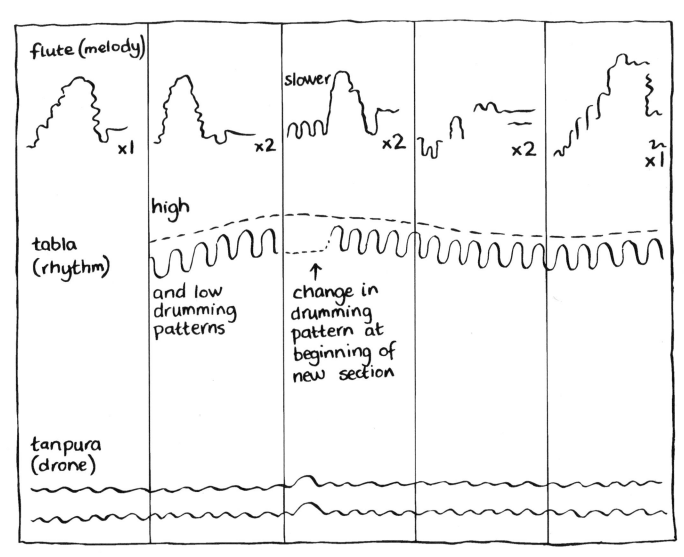

Make it clear that their sheets should show what is happening in the music, and whether they can hear drone, melody, rhythm, or a combination. They can pick up the appropriately coloured pen or pencil and add more detail whenever they notice it. The end results might look something like the illustration above (shown in black and white).

Suggest to the children that they might like to add written comments to the patterns representing the music (like the ones in the example above, but do not show this to them until they have finished). When they are satisfied that they have represented the raga to the best of their ability, discuss the different groups' interpretations and show them your own sheet, asking them to comment on this and the other versions. You might like to play the recording again while volunteers from one or more groups hold up their sheets for the rest of the class to follow.

If you are spreading this activity over two sessions, end the first session here.

Now tell the children that they are going to use their sheets as a graphic score for their own raga. Give out a range of tuned and untuned instruments to each group, and ask them to work out how to make the most appropriate use of them to play a raga. Remind them that their raga must include the three elements they have represented on their sheets: the drone, the melody and the rhythm. (The drone does not need to be played on a stringed instrument as in the recording, any tuned instrument can be used.) Ask the children to start and finish their melody part on a D, making sure the *pattern* of their melody echoes that of the raga they have heard; they can easily make it go up and down in the same way, and can also experiment with some simple embellishments to their tunes. The drone should also be played on or centred around a D.

Give the groups about 20 minutes to work on their ragas, encouraging them to make changes if they are not satisfied with the effect they are creating; they should, however, keep to the pattern of their graphic scores at all times. Tell them to practise their final versions once they have made all their decisions, then bring the groups back together to perform their ragas to the rest of the class. Record the performances if possible, then play the recordings and ask the class to evaluate what they hear (you might like to use the Responding to music sheet 135 for this). Conclude the session by playing the original recording again, and comparing it with the ragas the children have created. If you want them to write down their comparisons, they can use photocopiable sheet 133.

Suggestion(s) for extension

Children who have shown particular sensitivity in recreating the sound and structure of the 'Raga Bhimpalasi' can be asked to create their own note sequences, assigning particular moods and times of day to the new ragas they create. This activity also provides opportunities for those children who are having instrumental lessons to make use of their instrumental skills in a classroom context, perhaps playing increasingly complex variations on the sequence of notes for the raga.

Suggestion(s) for support

Some children will find it hard to grasp the complexity of the way in which the sequence of notes in the raga is used. It will help if you play them very short extracts from the recording and ask them to listen very carefully and then to sing along as you play them again. (This is actually the way that instrumental skills are taught in India using the singing voice.) Children who are having difficulty recreating the raga with instruments will find the drone the least demanding, but beware of dismissing this as an easy option: the drone is one of the most important features of the raga, and needs to be played with great sensitivity towards the other instruments.

Assessment opportunities

This activity provides opportunities to assess children's ability to represent and reproduce the sound and structure of a raga, to follow their own graphic score, to select and use instruments appropriately and to practise and present a performance of a finished piece.

Opportunities for IT

The 'Roland' range of keyboards have a built-in scale feature which allows you to re-tune each note. In this way, the notes of the Western scale can be 'bent' to give a more authentic Indian sound.

Display ideas

Copies of the children's pattern tracking sheets can be displayed alongside descriptions of both the original raga and their own versions. You could also display Indian fabrics, art and artefacts to set the music in context. Have a recording of the raga and the children's own versions available for the viewer to follow on the photocopiable sheets as they listen.

Reference to photocopiable sheets

Photocopiable sheet 142 is an analysis sheet used to record the structure of a piece of music using graphic notation. Sheet 133 invites children to compare two pieces of music. Sheet 135 is a listening response sheet which prompts children to think about certain aspects of the music that they hear.

Moving forward

You can repeat this activity using music from different cultures, and look for similarities and differences in structure and instrumentation. The exploration of musical structure and texture can also be developed further through the activity 'Listening collage' on page 48.

Pop, Rock and Jazz

This chapter is about 'the music of the people'. It takes you through pop and rock to an exploration of jazz structure and street rhythms. The chapter offers you a number of ways to capitalise on children's up-to-the-minute knowledge of the music scene. Pop music is the bridge between many children's school lives and the outside world, and is the one musical field in which they are generally the real experts. For once, they are the ones who can provide the knowledge, the vocabulary and the understanding that we may lack.

The beauty of popular music is its simplicity of design: the basic components of rhythm, melody and harmony within a recognisable overall structure are generally very easy to hear. The activities in this chapter focus on each of these components, giving you an opportunity to channel the children's knowledge and enthusiasm, and at the same time enhance their understanding, not only of their own favourite songs, but also of all the other music they hear.

TOP OF YOUR POPS

To enable children to listen analytically to familiar music and to develop their understanding of pop music.

†† *Pairs working in rotation, then whole class.*

🕐 *45 minutes (for each pair working in rotation over a week), then one or more 45-minute sessions (whole class).*

♪ *Easy.*

Previous skills/knowledge needed

It will help if the children have some previous experience of concentrated listening. The activity relies on the majority of children in the class having some knowledge of pop music.

Key background information

Children do not always realise how much they know about music. Yet for many of them, music forms a central component of their lives: on the radio, on the television, on the stereo system. They talk about it, they read about it, they dance to it and they play it at every opportunity, but they (and their teachers) hardly ever think of it as appropriate material for a classroom music lesson. This activity is designed to tap into the children's expertise and channel it in such a way that they become more aware of their own knowledge. The activity runs over a whole week (unless you have multiple cassette recorders and headphones, in which case all the pairs can work simultaneously), with pairs working in rotation over several days, followed by a presentation session at the end of the week.

Vocabulary

For once, it will be up to the children to supply this for you! The details will depend upon the types of music they choose.

Preparation

Again, the responsibility for this lies largely with the children. They will need to choose a partner to work with, agree on a piece of music to listen to, and decide who will bring it into school for the week. All you need to do is provide something for them to play their music on.

Resources needed

Children's own selections of pop music on CD or cassette, CD player or cassette player, headphones (if available), a range of writing materials, preferably including bright colours (for example, felt-tipped pens), paper, pictures and magazine articles about pop stars collected by the children (optional).

What to do

A few days before you start this activity, ask the children to decide in pairs on a pop song they would like to listen to and arrange for one of them to bring a recording of the song into school. If they like, they can also collect pictures and articles related to their chosen songs and performers.

Start the activity by explaining that each pair is going to give a presentation about their chosen song at the end of the week. They will begin their presentation by playing the song, then go on to tell the class about its main features. Their work for the presentation will focus on 'Twenty things you should know about... (title of their chosen song)'. Stress that they are describing the song, not the performer – this is

not an exercise in fan-club journalism!

During the week, give each pair about 45 minutes to listen to their song several times (using headphones if they are available), to decide on the twenty most significant things about it. These can be derived from reading about the music as well as listening to it if they like; and they can then record these on their sheet. Their comments might include 'It's got a great beat', 'It's really good for dancing to', 'The instruments take turns with the singer', or 'We like the way X changes the tone of his voice'. Each pair can decorate their sheet with their own pop-art illustrations or pictures from magazines. They could create and decorate their sheets using a computer (see 'Opportunities for IT').

Ask each pair to practise their presentation at least once (you might like to set aside additional time for this), making sure that both partners are fully involved. The presentations should be as exciting and as interesting as possible; you might like to suggest that they use a DJ-style of voice, or present themselves as reviewers from a music book or magazine.

When all the groups have done their preparation, set aside one or more blocks of time for the presentations. After each one, invite the rest of the class to ask the presenters questions about the song or the style of music. You might like to conclude the activity by holding a class disco, with each pair acting as DJs for the song they have been studying.

Suggestion(s) for extension

Children who clearly know a lot about pop music can include in their presentation a description of the style to which their chosen song belongs as well as a description of the song itself. You might like to suggest they prepare an additional sheet for this so that they can present 'Twenty things you should know about... (the particular style)'.

Some children may not be experts on pop styles, but may show an ability to describe their chosen songs in depth. You can challenge these children by asking them to justify or elaborate on the statements they make on their sheets. For example, they might be encouraged to write 'It's really good for dancing to because it's got a strong, steady beat', or 'The combination of jazz sounds and African rhythms makes this a really interesting piece'.

Suggestion(s) for support

Some children may not be at all familiar with pop music, and feel very left out of this activity if it is not handled sensitively. It will help them to learn about pop music styles if they are paired with a more expert partner, but they also need to be invited to demonstrate their own opinion or expertise. Ask them to describe three or four things that they like or dislike about the music, and incorporate these into their sheet.

Assessment opportunities

This activity enables you to monitor children's ability to listen analytically to familiar music and to describe what they hear using musical vocabulary, including specialist terms relating to particular musical styles.

Opportunities for IT

The children could use a word processor or desktop publishing package to write their list of 'Twenty things you should know about...' These could then be used to create overhead projector transparencies for their presentation to the rest of the class. The children will need to know how to make bullet points for their comments, alter the fonts and make the presentation fit neatly onto a limited number (probably two) of OHP slides. Where schools have access to more sophisticated software such as *Powerpoint*, older children could use this to design a paper or electronically-based presentation.

An alternative approach would be for children to make a multi-media presentation using authoring software. They could use snatches of the music recorded using a microphone attached to the computer or sampled from CD-ROMs. They could add text and pictures to extend the work. They could work in small groups with a limited number of linked screens to design their presentation. Much of the initial design work could be undertaken away from the computer.

Display ideas

Completed sheets can be displayed alongside photographs of pop stars and cuttings from popular music magazines. Interactive computer files set up by the children (see 'Opportunities for IT') can be opened for display.

Moving forward

This activity links very well with 'Chartbusters' in this chapter, in which the children compose their own pop song, and with 'Zein's tune' on page 74, which focuses on the familiar and unfamiliar in a Tunisian pop song. 'The style game' on page 46 invites the children to compare and comment on different styles of music. The idea of 'Twenty things you should know about...' can be used with any type of music – you might like to use it in conjunction with activities from the *Classical music* and *World music* chapters, or to incorporate it into some of the activities in the *Listening* chapter.

CHARTBUSTERS

*To build on and develop the children's awareness of
popular song structure through composition.*

🎻 *Groups of four to six.*

🕐 *Two 45-minute sessions.*

🎵 *Medium.*

Previous skills/knowledge needed

Any of the activities in the *Basic skills* chapter would provide
a good background to this activity, though none are essential.
It will help if the children have developed some confidence in
using their voices before doing this activity, and have
developed some rhythmic awareness.

Key background information

There are probably as many types of pop music as there are
classical, but making a few generalisations will give you a
useful structure to work with for this activity. The most
important components of pop songs (as of almost any other
music) are *melody* (the tune), *harmony* (the notes which are
combined with the tune – in pop songs this usually comprises
a bass line and a sequence of chords), *rhythm* (usually
provided in pop songs by a drum kit plus a few other
percussion instruments) and, of course, *lyrics* (words). A
high proportion of popular songs are based on multiple
repetitions of these features, with only minor changes being
made from the beginning of the song to the end. Some pop
songs follow the folk structure of verse-chorus-verse-chorus,
while others belong more to the jazz tradition, with the
beginning and end being joined by a 'middle eight' – an eight-
bar section where the tune takes a new turn (see the 'Middle
8' activity on page 98 for more details).

However, this activity relies on the children's *implicit*
knowledge of pop music, not on detailed analysis. Do not
worry if they seem to know a lot more than you, just make
use of it!

Vocabulary

Rhythm, melody, tune, harmony, bass, beat, lyrics.

Preparation

A few days before you carry out this activity, listen to some
pop music and see whether you can pick out the beat of the
music. There may be some complex rhythmic patterns, but
there is probably a very simple beat underlying them. Now
try singing along with the tune (the melody) – is it predictable?
Can you guess what will happen next even if you do not
know it? Is it repeated throughout the song? Lastly, listen to
the bass line and see if you can sing or hum along with that.
This can be quite difficult as it is sometimes hard to
disentangle from other elements of the song; but with certain
types of music, for example rock 'n' roll, it is very easy. Copy
evaluation sheets 151 and 152 for each group if required.

Resources needed

CD or cassette player, blank cassette (optional), recordings
of pop music – either your own, or brought in by the children
– paper and pens/pencils, one drum per group and a further
selection of tuned and untuned instruments, including
electronic instruments and amplification if available.

What to do

Session one

Divide the class into groups of four to six before you start
the activity, but do not give out the instruments. Select three
or four samples of pop music and play brief excerpts of them
to the class – not more than a minute from each song. With
each one, invite the children to tap or clap to the rhythm,
and ask them to keep the rhythm going when you stop the

MUSIC

music. Once they are doing this successfully, give out one drum per group and ask each group to invent a pop-song rhythm of its own, using tapping and clapping in time with the drum. Give them five minutes to do this – a limited time can often be very productive, and they will have opportunities to add further details to the rhythm later.

Stop the groups and talk briefly about the subjects and words of the songs they heard at the beginning of the session. (Do not ask them to demonstrate their rhythms to each other yet, as they are likely to forget their own when they hear each others'.) Ask the children to add some words (lyrics) to their rhythms. The lyrics can be either spoken or sung, rhymed or unrhymed. Give them another ten minutes or so for this, then give out the tuned instruments and ask them to add the final component – the bass line. Ask them to choose a sequence of low notes and repeat them again and again, with slight changes if they like, throughout the song. Give them about 20 minutes to work on their combinations of lyrics, rhythm and bass, then ask each group to perform their pop song. Invite the groups to comment on each others' work, and to suggest ways in which each composition might be developed. (They could use photocopiable sheet 151 as a guide for their comments.) Trust the children's knowledge of pop music to guide their judgements. Conclude this session by asking the groups to write down their songs in some way that will help them to remember all the components – the words, the rhythm and the bass line.

Session two
Start this session by reminding the children of the different components of their songs, and of the comments they made on each others' work. Give them about 20 minutes to revise and practise. They can add instruments if they wish to enhance the melody, the harmony, the rhythm, or all three.

Groups that have produced spoken lyrics can either keep their composition as a rap, or now put a tune to the words. Remind the children that *practising* involves selecting the parts where they have difficulties and working on them, not just going right through the song again and again. When they are ready, ask each group to perform to the rest of the class. If you can amplify the performances, so much the better. It is a good idea to record each performance and invite the children to evaluate it. (You can use photocopiable sheet 152 for this.) You might like to add more spice to the performance by making it into a classroom talent show, perhaps bringing in judges in the form of other teachers or another class.

Suggestion(s) for extension
Children who show talent as singer/songwriters can be 'commissioned' by you or the class to write a song on a particular theme, or for a particular combination of vocalists and instruments.

Suggestion(s) for support
Some children will find it difficult to come up with any ideas at all, particularly if they lack confidence and familiarity with the world of pop music. Try inviting them to sing along (in groups) with one of the recordings used at the beginning of the activity, perhaps adding their own percussion rhythms. They could then try adding a new verse of their own.

Assessment opportunities
This activity demonstrates children's awareness of song structure, and their ability to build on this to create their own songs. The activity also presents opportunities to look at performance style, for example, whether the group members keep in time with each other, can remember and sustain their rhythm, and can control the quality of their voices.

Opportunities for IT

The children could use a keyboard or specific computer music program such as *Music Explorer* or *Music Box* to compose their song. They could begin by setting up and playing a repeating drum. A bass line could be added in a similar way. Once this has been set up, they can then compose the tune as well, selecting appropriate instruments and a structure. The whole activity could be tailored to the age and ability of the children – from the simple composition, using one rhythm, tune and instrument, to the more sophisticated using complex rhythms and a range of instruments. This type of activity gives children opportunities to experiment with drafting and re-drafting a musical composition.

Display ideas

Photographs of the class 'pop groups' can be displayed alongside photographs of real pop groups and an explanation of the essential components of pop songs: melody, harmony and rhythm. Children's evaluations of their own compositions and performances can also be displayed.

Reference to photocopiable sheets

Sheets 151 and 152 are evaluation sheets that invite children to reflect on their own compositions and performances.

Moving forward

This activity links particularly well with the activity 'Middle 8' in this chapter. Once you have done 'Middle 8', it is worth returning to 'Chartbusters' to give the children an opportunity to apply the knowledge they have gained. The performance skills developed in this activity can be used in 'Performance poetry' on page 34, while the way a popular song is structured is explored further in the next activity in this chapter, 'Pattern tracking'.

PATTERN TRACKING

To develop children's awareness of musical structure through listening to jazz.

†† *Whole class.*
🕐 *30 minutes.*
🎵 *Medium.*

Previous skills/knowledge needed

It would be helpful if the children have had some experience of exploring musical structure. ('Going round in circles' in the Key Stage 1 book explores musical structure at a fairly simple level.) At Key Stage 2, 'Musical printout' and 'Journey lines' on pages 42 and 44 can be used as a good basis for this activity. Experience of graphic notation would be useful (see the activity 'Graphic notation – instant composition' on page 108), though it can also be introduced through this activity.

Key background information

All music, from any part of the world, has a discernible structure, often using repeating patterns. In Western popular, classical and folk music this often takes the form of two or more sections which alternate with each other. The song used in this activity, 'Java Jive' (available on the cassette that can be purchased to accompany this book) has the typical jazz structure of: Introduction, Tune A, Tune A, Tune B, Tune A. ('Java' is an American word for coffee.) If you do not have the cassette, you can use any other piece of music with a similar structure. It does not have to be jazz, although if you intend to move on to the 'Middle 8' activity (see 'Moving forward') you will need to use a jazz piece.

Vocabulary

Pattern, repeat, solo, jazz, structure.

Preparation

Listen to 'Java Jive' (or your own choice of music) and identify the Introduction, Tune A and Tune B. Make an enlarged copy (A3) of pattern tracking sheet 142 for each child and one to attach to a white board or flip chart.

Resources needed

Recording of 'Java Jive' by The Ink Spots (MCA), or your own choice of music, cassette player, one A3 copy of photocopiable sheet 142 for each child, coloured pencils, white board or flip chart, marker pens.

What to do

Play 'Java Jive' to the class; they will almost certainly love it, and will probably start moving in time to it as soon as it starts. Play it again, and ask them to join in with as much of the song as they can – they should have no difficulty with the beginning.

Now ask the children to tell you what they could hear in the song:

▲ What combination of voices and instruments did they notice?

▲ How did the song start?

▲ What did the different voices do?

Ask them to think about these questions while they listen to the music again. Were they right? Is there anything they can add?

Now look at the chart on the board, and ask them if they can tell you what should be in the first section. They may be able to tell you straight away that it is a guitar introduction, but if not, play the beginning of the song again. Ask the children to suggest how this might be represented on the chart. It might look something like the illustration below (draw the guitar line fairly low down, so it can continue below the voices if you want to look at *texture* later):

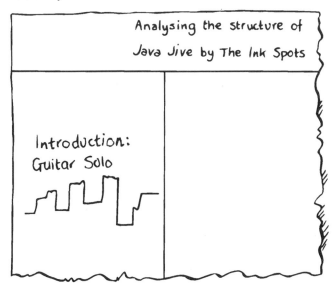

Now ask the children how you should fill in the next section; this is where the voices come in. Listen to the music again if necessary, then add this section to the chart. Call this 'Tune A'.

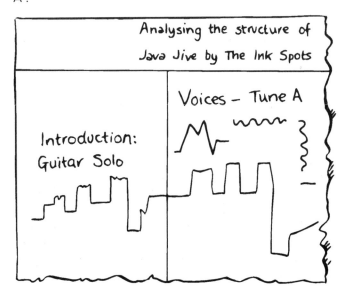

With 'I love java, sweet and hot', Tune A starts again – play it for the children to hear, then add it to the third section of the chart, *as a repeat of Tune A*.

Now the tune changes ('Slip me a slug'). Discuss with the children how they might represent this, but do not fill it in on the chart. Call this part 'Tune B' (this section is called the 'middle eight' which you might like to mention if you are planning to move on to the 'Middle 8' activity). Ask if they can hear where Tune A ('I like coffee') comes back in at the end. Describe this sequence of tunes as a *musical structure*.

Now play the whole song again, and ask the children to raise their hands every time the tune changes. Remind them that 'Tune A' is played twice before 'Tune B' comes in.

Write the headings 'Tune B' and 'Tune A' in the fourth and fifth sections of the chart on the board, then give each child a copy of photocopiable sheet 142 and ask them to complete it in their own way. Remind them of the ideas you discussed while you were listening to the song, and remind them that they need to draw lines or symbols to represent the guitar and voices. Play the song several more times as they do this, and point out where the different sections start. You may need to give them quite a lot of time to complete their charts.

Conclude the session by asking the children to follow their charts through as you play the music a final time. Ask them to tell you the sequence: Introduction, Tune A, Tune A, Tune B, Tune A.

Suggestion(s) for extension

Some children may be able to add details of the musical *texture* to their charts. For example, they could show that the guitar keeps playing all the way through, and that there is a solo voice which is supported by a backing group – this could be shown in the number of symbols they use to represent the singers, while the guitar part could be shown as a continuous line right across the chart, with no variation in width. They could go on to use the same chart to analyse different pieces of music.

Suggestion(s) for support

Children who do not feel confident representing the sections of the music on their charts may need to listen several more times, and just raise their hands when they hear a different tune come in.

Assessment opportunities

This activity offers opportunities to observe children's awareness of musical structure, and their ability to represent it using graphic notation.

Opportunities for IT

The children could use the pre-programmed musical sequences in software such as *Compose World* to create and experiment with musical structures. Other software will allow children to compose and program in their own structures and then use them in a similar way.

Display ideas

Completed analysis sheets (photocopiable sheet 142) can be displayed along with written responses (sheet 135) to the music. Pictures and photographs could also be displayed showing the theme of the song.

Reference to photocopiable sheet

Sheet 142 invites children to analyse the *structure* of a piece of music by dividing it into sections, and then mapping what happens in each section. It offers them an opportunity to use graphic notation (that is, informal symbols of their own choosing) to represent the music they listen to. The sheet can be used equally well with any style of music.

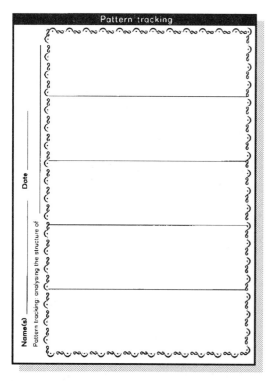

Moving forward

This activity links directly with the next activity in this chapter 'Middle 8' which makes further use of the knowledge of song structure the children have developed here. It also leads onto 'Listening collage' on page 48, and 'Recreating a raga' on page 86 which uses the same analysis sheet.

🎧 MIDDLE 8

To develop children's awareness of song structure in jazz and pop music, and to enhance their compositional skills.

†† *Whole class, then individuals, pairs or groups.*

🕐 *Two 60-minute sessions.*

♪ *Advanced.*

Previous skills/knowledge needed

This activity follows on directly from 'Pattern tracking', building on the understanding of structure developed in that activity and using the same song as a starting-point. The children will need to be fairly confident in using their voices and in working with song lyrics: 'Chartbusters' in this chapter would provide particularly useful experience for this. It will also help if they have some experience of counting sets of beats. 'Stars in your eyes' on page 106 provides this as does 'Beat sums and bar lines' on page 110.

Key background information

The term 'middle eight' comes from the world of jazz. It refers to the set of eight bars which come in the middle of a song or tune, bringing in a new musical theme after the main tune has been introduced. These bars are sandwiched between two sections of the main tune – hence the term 'middle'. In the song 'Java Jive', used here, the middle eight has already been identified in the 'Pattern tracking' activity as 'Tune B'. (If you do not have the cassette, choose any song which has a middle section of this type, see 'Preparation'.) Middle eight sections do not usually occur in straightforward verse-chorus pop songs (for example 'Ob-la-di, Ob-la-da' by The Beatles), but if you play any of the popular songs from the 1930s or 1940s, you will almost certainly find a middle eight in each one. It will probably begin at the point where you find you cannot remember what happens next in the song! In some, the middle eight follows much the same pattern as the main tune, while in others, the new tune takes off in a completely different direction. In the song used here, 'Java Jive' the middle eight is a completely new tune (it begins with the words 'Slip me a slug').

Vocabulary

Jazz, beats, bars, middle eight.

Preparation

Listen to 'Java Jive' on the cassette (or your own choice of song) and make sure you can identify the middle eight ('Tune B'). Refer back to 'Pattern tracking' if you are unsure of this. Listen to a range of other popular songs (anything from the 1920s to the 1990s is fine), and try to work out whether each has a middle-eight section or not. Choose two or three of the songs, making sure that at least one has a middle-eight section, and have these ready to play at the beginning

---

of the activity. Get out the pattern tracking sheets the children have already completed. Have some tuned and untuned instruments available (see 'Resources needed') and writing materials to use with the sheets. If you would like the children to evaluate either their composition or their performance, make copies of photocopiable sheets 151 or 154 and 155 as appropriate.

Resources needed

Cassette player, recording of 'Java Jive' (on the cassette), or your own choice of music, and a selection of other popular songs, completed pattern tracking sheets, evaluation sheets (as above) if required, plain paper, writing materials, a selection of tuned and untuned instruments for individuals or groups to use them if they wish – they may not use any of them, but they need to be available.

What to do
Session one

Without giving out any sheets or instruments, play 'Java Jive' to the class and invite them to join in with the song. They may not yet know all the words, but the more times they hear it, the more they will find they can remember. Play it through again, then ask the children what happens to the tune at the line 'Slip me a slug from the wonderful jug' (or at the beginning of the middle eight in your chosen song). They may simply say that the tune changes, or they may remember that this is what they called 'Tune B' in the previous activity. Tell them that this section is called the middle eight, and ask them whether they can work out why. Once you have

established that it is a sequence of eight bars in the middle of the song, count through the section as you play it again. You will need to count eight sets of four beats, starting like this:

1	2	3 4	1	2	3 4
Slip me a slug _		from the wonderful jug	_ _		

Now play the other songs you chose in your preparation, and ask the children whether each has a middle-eight section, and to identify it, if it has. Give out the pattern tracking sheets and ask them to show you where they have drawn the middle eight for the song studied in the previous activity (this will be the section they have identified as Tune B). Play it through one more time so that they can follow it on their sheets.

Explain to the children that they are going to invent a new middle eight for the song, making new lyrics of their own to follow on from the first part of the song. This can be done either individually, in pairs or in small groups (you can either decide this yourself, or give them a free choice) but *everyone* must be involved in both composing *and* performing their new section. They can choose whether or not to use instruments: they may want to have a rhythmic or melodic accompaniment to their composition, or they may just want to use voices. Remind the children that the section they are composing must last for only eight bars: eight sets of four beats. Give out the plain paper and ask them to write down their new lyrics, adding note-names if they have worked them out on instruments; if they have thought of accompanying rhythms, they could indicate these too. Finish this session

with a demonstration of work in progress if it seems appropriate (you may wish to leave all demonstration until the final performance).

Session two

Start this session by playing 'Java Jive' (or the music you have chosen) to the class again, to remind the children of the framework in which they are working. Then give them enough time to complete and practise their compositions, focusing on the way in which the tune they have invented fits the rhythm of their lyrics. Ask them to think about their *performance* skills as they are practising (they may use photocopiable sheets 154 and 155 later to evaluate their performance). When they are ready, set up a classroom performance where each new middle eight is performed at the appropriate point in the song. Do this by playing the cassette for all the class to sing along to for each performance, but turning the volume down during the middle-eight section so the individual's or group's own versions can be heard each time. As well as giving them a 'backing group' for the rest of the song, this will help them to hear whether or not they have made their new middle eight the right length (that is, eight bars).

After the performances, ask the children to evaluate their own and each others' work. You might choose to use a further session for them to revise and practise their compositions in the light of these evaluations, leading to a final performance; or they might be able to incorporate these improvements straight away. As a follow-up, you can ask the children to reflect on their composition or on their performance, using photocopiable sheets 151 or 154 and 155.

Suggestion(s) for extension

Children who have been particularly successful with this activity can compose a new middle eight for other songs. Alternatively, they can add vocal harmonies to their compositions, or add rhythmic and/or melodic accompaniments on instruments.

Suggestion(s) for support

Some children will find it hard to grasp the concept of eight bars, or eight sets of four beats. It will help if you count through the middle-eight section of 'Java Jive' with them several times, then ask them to count through on their own. Children who find it hard to create lyrics or a melody of their own will benefit from working with a more confident partner, so that they can learn how musical choices are made.

Assessment opportunities

You can assess the children's developing awareness of musical structure and their compositional skills. You will also be able to note their performance skills.

Opportunities for IT

The children could write the lyrics on a word processor and add note-names and symbols for percussion above or below the words.

Display ideas

You and the children could set up a 'Middle Eight' display incorporating the words of a range of songs with the middle-eight section missing. Viewers could then be invited to supply the missing lyrics. Alternatively, you could display the words of the middle-eight section only, and invite viewers to guess which songs they come from. The display could also include recordings of the songs, complete with middle-eight sections, against which suggestions could be checked.

Reference to photocopiable sheets

Sheets 151, 154 and 155 invite the children to evaluate their own skills in composing and performing.

Moving forward

Once you have done this activity, you might like to revisit 'Chartbusters' in this chapter at a higher level, asking the children to incorporate a middle eight into their songs. Alternatively, you could move on to another composition-based activity, such as 'Composing with voices' on page 37, using the skills which have been developed here.

Pop, Rock and Jazz

STREETWISE

To develop children's rhythmic skills and their awareness of complex rhythmic patterns. To promote their performance skills.

†† *Whole class.*

🕐 *60 minutes (or two shorter sessions).*

♫ *Advanced.*

Previous skills/knowledge needed

This activity builds on children's earliest explorations with sound and combines these with their increasing understanding of rhythmic patterns. 'Something for nothing' in the *Using Instruments* chapter of the KS1 book lays the foundations for this activity with its rhythmic use of 'found' instruments. The children should have had experience in keeping a beat together and playing more than one rhythm at a time. 'African polyrhythms' on page 80 would be a useful preparation for this. 'Performance poetry' on page 34 is another activity where the rhythmic use of words is investigated.

Key background information

Playing instruments made from everyday materials is quite a common phenomenon in many cultures. Samba instruments in Latin America are traditionally made from junk. Steel pans are made from oil drums that the American army left littering the Caribbean. In the days of apartheid, black miners were banned from using drums so took to playing rhythms on the wellington boots that they wore for work. The idea of creating percussion instruments from rubbish is used by a group called Stomp (also known as Yes/No People). They started off busking in the streets with whatever rubbish came to hand – dustbins, broom handles, carrier bags, paper cups – and their popularity has led to an upsurge of interest in 'rhythms of the street'. This music shows that it is not the type of instruments you use that turn a collection of sounds into a performance, but the sharpness and concentration with which you play them, and how inventive you can be with them.

Vocabulary

Pulse, beat, rhythm.

Preparation

A few days before the lesson, ask the children to bring in some crackly carrier bags and any other junk materials which you feel would be appropriate. Ask your colleagues (including the caretaker) for any spare broom handles. Look around your classroom and decide what things would stand up to being used as percussion instruments if banged or shaken and what you want to put off-limits. You may like to split the activity into two sessions to give the children more time to focus on the activity.

Resources needed

Anything that you can bang, shake, scrape, rustle – for example, broom handles, old baked bean tins, carrier bags – blank cassette, cassette player.

What to do

With the children standing in a circle ask them to keep a steady pulse with their feet. Emphasise that they must not rush and they do not need to be loud, just steady. Start counting in fours, tapping on the first of every four beats: 1, 2, 3, 4, 1, 2, 3, 4. Explain that you are going to teach them the introduction to a rhythm piece.

Still keeping a steady pulse ask them to stamp and shout the first beat '1', '2, 3, 4' then, next time round, the first and second beats '1, 2,' '3, 4'. On the next round they say a quick '1-2-3' into a 'dada dum' rhythm with the 3, 4 beats still silent. Finally, the fourth time it is a steady '1, 2, 3, 4'. The rhythm could be represented like this:

● 1	....	~~~~~~	~~~~~~
● 1	● 2	....	....
●●● 1 2	● 3	~~~~~~	~~~~~~
● 1	● 2	● 3	● 4

This will form the introduction.

Now teach the group this rhyme:

1	2	3	4
Hey	kid	think you	know it?
Step	right	here and	show it

This is the basic rhythm which is going to be split up between the members of the class. Divide the class into six groups and give one line of the rhyme to each one (see below). Ask each group to think up a distinctive body sound. They are going to say their part of the rhyme while playing the same rhythm with their body sound. The different lines of the rhyme are as follows:

Group 1	Hey,	— —	—
Group 2	Hey	kid, —	—
Group 3	—	— think you	know it?
Group 4	Step,	— —	—
Group 5	Step	right here,	—
Group 6	—	— here and	show it.

Give the children time to practise on their own before trying to put all the different parts together. Tell them to say the

words loudly with their body sounds, but to count the 'empty' beats silently. When they have practised, bring the groups back together. Tapping out a steady pulse to keep them in time, start with everyone doing the introduction you learned earlier using voices and feet, then go straight into the rhyme, with one group joining in after another, repeating their lines again and again. Try out different ways of performing the rhyme: you might have each line said on its own first, then all the parts brought together; or you might fade groups in and out.

If you are doing this activity over two sessions, end the first one here.

Consolidate what you have done so far by performing the rhyme through two or three times with the different groups saying their parts. When you feel they are confident, give out the instruments that have been collected. The following instruments should be used for the following groups:
▲ broomsticks for the 'hey' group;
▲ baked bean tins for the 'hey kid' group;
▲ carrier bags for the 'think you know it' group;
▲ things which can be scraped for the 'step' group.
▲ things which can be shaken for the 'step right here' group; and finally,
▲ dustpan and brush or spoons for the 'here and show it' group.

The 'instruments' should only be played along with the voices and the 'empty' beats should still be counted silently. Again, give the groups some time to practise separately, then bring them back together.

Discuss ways in which you could vary the performance using different dynamics, and different combinations and types of voices and instruments. What difference does it make if you change the instruments that are used? What happens if you change the voice quality? Think about making the piece exciting to look at. Use starting positions for each group or individual (for instance, leaning on the broom handles) and try to incorporate movement into the rhythms; simple costume such as 'shades' and baseball caps would add instant atmosphere.

Make a recording of the performances for the children to listen to.

Suggestion(s) for extension
Ask the more confident children to make up their own words and rhythms and put on a 'Streetwise' performance for the rest of the class. Challenge these children by asking them to take a part on their own; this extends their ability to hold a rhythm independently.

Suggestion(s) for support
If a child is finding the activity hard, ask her or him to play the 'Hey 2, 3, 4' line as this is the easiest one to keep going. It will also help if you position them next to someone who is confident. Often a child who is having difficulty responds to being given more time to practise.

Assessment opportunities
This activity gives the opportunity for observing and hearing how well individuals play a rhythm, both within a group and independently, and to note their developing awareness of complex rhythmic patterns. It also enables you to monitor their performance skills.

Display ideas
The sight of children playing broomsticks and carrier bags can be eye-catching! Take photographs of the sessions and ask the children to make written explanations of what is going on and how the sounds were created. Put these in the music display area next to the recording of their performance.

Moving forward
Go busking around the school! Alternatively, do the activity again using increasingly complex rhythms – you could try starting the groups at different times to create cross-rhythms.

Notation

Notation is the means by which music is recorded so that someone other than the original composer can play it. For many people, music notation is solely the unintelligible little dots seen in music books. All too often, people are heard to say 'I'm not musical – I can't read music'. This chapter is the absolute reverse of this sentiment. It is significant that the National Curriculum document refers to 'notations', not notation; by this it means a range of different ways in which children can record their own compositions. Some of those ways are represented here, but it is important to remember that the children can invent new forms of notation which would be equally acceptable within the teaching of National Curriculum music. Often, this informal notation can add greatly to the children's understanding of and creativity with music, as well as being highly enjoyable and non-threatening to work with.

Formal notation (the little dots) is represented in this chapter in a way that can be easily used and understood by non-specialists. Children love learning about it and it can boost their view of themselves as musicians. While notation is generally used to record what has already been composed, it can be used as a means of instant composition, by asking them to use symbols to create a composition before it is actually played. This can be effective for teachers who feel worried about teaching composition, as the activity can be very tightly structured, while allowing for the children's ideas and creativity to be developed so that they think about their compositions.

COLOUR NOTATION

To introduce and use the concept of using colour as a form of notation.

†† *Whole class divided into pairs or groups of five.*

🕐 *40 minutes.*

♫ *Easy.*

Previous skills/knowledge needed

Familiarity with playing tuned percussion would support this activity, although it could also be used to familiarise children with this skill. 'Introducing scales' on page 23 explains how to share a limited number of tuned percussion instruments, such as chime bars or xylophones, among a class of 30, while still enabling all the children to take part.

Key background information

Notation is about representing a sound by a symbol that can be recognised by those reading it. In this case the symbol is a series of coloured squares, drawn on paper or using Unifix cubes, where each colour represents a different note. This method can be adapted to suit the level of complexity that you are using. At the simplest level, three coloured squares could be used to represent three different notes. These can be arranged and played as many times and in as many different ways as the composer wishes.

Vocabulary

Notes, note names, melody, scale, notation.

Preparation

Collect all the tuned percussion that you can find. This will probably be a variety of instruments in different conditions of repair. Do not discount the old xylophone with only five bars, nor the single chime bars that do not seem to fit in. As far as you can, you will need at least three, and ideally five, different notes for each group. Even if the notes are just a different pitch, for example a high and a low sounding G, they can be used. The number in the groups, and in some cases the number of groups, will depend on how many sets of notes you can collect. It is possible to do the lesson with half the class – the noise from the playing will be very quiet and even on occasions, tuneful. Groups of five are used here.

For each group of children, whether they are groups of two or five, you will need five different notes, ideally C, D, E, F, G, either from individual chime bars or a xylophone. Find, buy or make sets of small coloured square or circular stickers which are to be used for notation. Attach the colour stickers to the instruments, covering up the place where the note name is shown. Use the same colour for each note name. For example, all 'C's could be green, all 'D's could be purple and so on. Prepare the first piece of music that the children are going to play by drawing a series of eight coloured squares onto paper. Only use three different colours/notes.

Resources needed

Sets of five notes, ideally C, D, E, F, G, one set of beaters, and one set of stickers per group, pencils, paper, adhesive or sticky tape, coloured pencils.

What to do

Arrange the children into the groups and seat each one around a set of notes. Introduce the first piece of music that you have prepared. Explain to the class that you are going to point to each colour/note and, taking it in turns, you want each child to play the tune. The rest of the group can help them. (If they are not used to playing a xylophone in groups, quickly revise the work of passing a beater from one player to the next.) Ask the children to number themselves from one to five. All the number ones in the groups play the tune and then pass the beater onto their next door neighbours – the number twos. If there are only two in a group, then each child will play more than once until all the children in the class have had a turn.

When the class has become accustomed to the idea of following the coloured squares, explain to the children that they are going to compose their own tunes using exactly the same system. Ask the groups to split themselves into two groups. One part of the group will compose and write down the tune, drawing and colouring in the squares just as you did, while the other part will play it twice each. This could be a suitable time to introduce two more colours so that they can compose their tunes using five notes instead of three.

Give the groups five minutes working time and then ask them to swap so that they get a chance to compose/play. To finish the session, have a grand performance of all the children's tunes.

Suggestion(s) for extension

If some children find this activity easy ask them to think of ways of making their tune more interesting: perhaps using quicker notes in some places; showing loud or soft; how a particular part of the tune can be repeated. There are no definitive rules, so they can use their own ideas to add different effects.

Introduce the idea of writing a tune for two parts (using two beaters to play on one or even two instruments for a showing at the end of the lesson).

Notation

Suggestion(s) for support

If some children are finding the activity hard, it could be either that they do not understand and cannot follow the notation, or that they cannot find the notes on their instrument quickly enough to keep up with the music. Explain and demonstrate again what you want them to do, using the sheet with the three coloured squares. Ask one child to point at the music while you play. Check that the child's instrument is arranged in a way that is easy to play, then go through the music *very* slowly so that he or she has plenty of time. If necessary, make the music shorter or suggest that the child can learn it in small chunks.

Assessment opportunities

This activity provides the opportunity to assess the children's ability to use colour as a form of notation, and their skill at playing instruments.

Opportunities for IT

The notation could be produced on the computer, though a colour printer would be needed. The children could use a drawing package with a pre-set grid in the background into which they place the coloured squares (shown by different shades of grey here). The teacher could set up a bank of squares around the drawing area from which children select the appropriate colour, duplicate it and drag it to the position. This activity works best if the background grid is displayed and the *'snap to grid'* option selected. A second row of squares could be added underneath for a second part to the tune.

Software such as *My World* could be used to make the same grid, with children dragging coloured squares from the reservoir of shapes along the side.

Display ideas

The notation sheets make a colourful display that can be greatly enhanced by an explanation of what the children were doing and photographs of the session. With all notation it is important to have instruments displayed nearby so that children can be invited to play the music that has been written.

Moving forward

If you wish to explore colour in notation further, the activity 'Graphic notation – instant composition' in this chapter uses symbols and colour. If you wish to look at ways of notating melody, 'Beat sums and bar lines', also in this chapter, introduces formal notation.

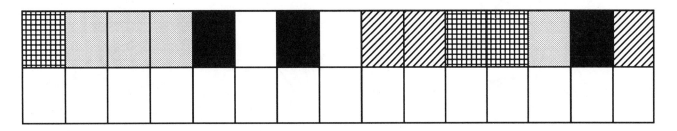

STARS IN YOUR EYES

To develop the ability to read and devise complex notation using a grid.

†† *Session one: whole class.*
Sessions two and three: groups of four.

🕐 *Three 30-minute sessions.*

♫ *Easy.*

Previous skills/knowledge needed

'Grid notation' in the Key Stage 1 book introduces the concept of working with a grid as a means to structure notation. Children will need experience of playing to a steady beat and playing sounds together. 'Controlling tempo' on page 21 would help to provide this. The activity 'Graphic notation – instant composition' in this chapter develops the idea of representing sounds with abstract symbols as part of the notation.

Key background information

Notation is the concept of representing sounds by a set of symbols. Children greatly enjoy notating work that they have composed themselves, using either *formal notation* (little dots that you find in music books), or *informal notation* (such as represented here). The great advantage of informal notation is that it can be used in a variety of ways, simple or complex, to notate what they have already played, or as a structured form of composing.

Vocabulary

Pulse, steady rhythm, notation, symbol.

Preparation

Prepare a grid on an A3 sheet of paper, or use an enlarged copy of photocopiable sheet 143. If you are going to use instruments for this activity collect together enough (tuned or untuned) for one per child. If this is not possible, the activity can work just as well with half the group having instruments and the other using body percussion (claps, slaps, clicks or yells). To avoid World War III breaking out, you would be wise to swap instruments half way through the activity to enable everyone to experience the instruments. Prepare one copy of sheet 143 for every four children.

Resources needed

One enlarged (A3 sized) copy of photocopiable sheet 143, enough (A4 sized) copies for one per four children, instruments if desired, felt-tipped pens or thick, coloured pencils, marker pens.

What to do

Session one

Seat the children so that they can see the enlarged grid. Explain that they are going to play every square. Start a steady pulse by tapping three fingers on the palm of your hand and ask the children to join in with you. As they do, they will often speed up a bit – remind them to keep the pulse steady and to relax into it. When this has been achieved, point to each square of the grid in time to the pulse, one beat per square. Start at the top left-hand corner and read it as you would a book, returning to the beginning of the next line, as you reach the end of each one.

When they have played the grid through a couple of times give a marker pen to one child. Ask her or him to draw a star on the grid wherever he or she likes. Repeat this with seven more children, reminding them that only one star is allowed in each square. Make sure that the first square of each line is given a star, as otherwise it is very difficult to play.

Ask the children to decide whether the star is a clap or a stamp. Point to the grid as before, but this time ask the children to clap or stamp when there is a star in the square. If there is no star they 'play the silence' by either clapping the air, or beating one pulse with palms facing upwards.

When you reach the end of the grid ask the children which part was the hardest to play. If they say the end of the line, practise that part particularly and remind them to quickly move their eyes back to the beginning of the next line. This time ask a child who can keep a steady beat to be the conductor. Tell them to point in the time of the pulse to the different squares, while the other children play.

Once the children are familiar with this way of playing you can notate the whole of the grid. Ask them to think up two more simple symbols, maybe a circle and squiggle. Decide what they represent. Ask them to draw in two or three of each symbol. If you want to have silent squares (squares with no sound) you will need to make sure that some are left blank. Now ask one child to conduct this new composition.

Session two

When you feel the children are familiar with this way of notation, ask them to work in groups of four. Give out a copy of photocopiable sheet 143 to each group. Tell the children that they are going to think up their own symbols and sounds to create their own piece of music. As a group they need to decide where to put the signs on the grid and also whether they wish to leave silences (blank squares). If they have not had much experience at this sort of activity, encourage them by saying that a simple sound played well is just as musical as a complicated one played in a mediocre way. Give them five to seven minutes to work out and write down the signs. Once they have done this, ask them to show you some examples of their sounds and symbols. Inform them that they are going to have another five to seven minutes to practise the piece before performing it to the class.

When they perform the piece it is often useful to have one child conducting the group by pointing to each square while keeping to a steady pulse.

Suggestion(s) for extension

If the class are finding this activity easy, widen the boundaries either by restricting what they can do, for instance using body percussion, or giving them more freedom and asking them to compose a piece using any stimulus or instrument they like, then using the grid to notate and record it.

Suggestion(s) for support

If some children are finding this activity difficult, reinforce the idea of reading the grid, by asking those who are finding it hard to take it in turns to be the conductor and point to the squares, while the rest of the group plays the piece. Alternatively, you could ask them to use a single line of four squares as their grid.

Assessment opportunities

This activity gives you the opportunity to assess the children's ability to read notation and play a steady rhythm when another three rhythms are being followed. You can assess either the class as a whole, or individuals.

Opportunities for IT

The children could use a drawing package with a four-by-four grid and add their symbols into the grid. They could design their symbols using the drawing package, use symbols

Session three

As the children grow more confident with this way of working, introduce the idea of playing the grid four ways at a time. Seat the children so that four are sitting one on each side of the paper on which the grid is written, facing inwards (see illustration above).

Each child will play the music in the order it is *as they look at it*. This means that every child will be playing a different order of symbols and, therefore, sounds according to where they are sitting. The children may find it hard to play all at the same time and maintain their notation reading. If this is the case, start with two children facing each other over the grid playing the piece, while the other two point to the symbols or keep a steady pulse.

★	⇓	♥	★
⇓		♥	
★		♥	⇓
⇓	★	♥	★

that are part of a font style such as 'Symbol' or 'Wingdings' or create simple picture symbols. A grid could be set up as a starting file and saved to disk so that children can retrieve it easily and use it for their own notation. Similar activities can be undertaken using software such as *Compose World*.

The activity could be extended by using multi-media authoring software and linking the symbols on the grid to a set of recorded sounds, made by using a microphone attached to the computer. When each symbol is clicked by the user the sound is played by the software. It should also be possible to set up the grid so that it plays automatically. Different groups could then make up their own notation grids and use a common set of recorded sounds so that a whole range of rhythms can presented and played from the same set of sounds.

Display ideas
The finished grids of the different groups make excellent interactive displays especially if there is an explanation (preferably by the children) of what, how and why it was done. If a set of appropriate instruments is supplied, you can invite people to have a go at playing the notations that have been composed.

Reference to photocopiable sheet
Photocopiable sheet 143 is of a four-by-four grid on which the notation is written.

GRAPHIC NOTATION – INSTANT COMPOSITION

To develop the concept of graphic notation and use it as a form of composing.

†† *Whole class, then groups of four or five.*

🕐 *45 minutes.*

♫ *Medium.*

Previous skills/knowledge needed
Familiarity with the concept of representing a sound by a symbol is required for this activity. 'Stars in your eyes' in this chapter provides this. The concept of abstract patterns and shapes representing sounds is examined in 'Graphic notation' from the *Notation* chapter in the Key Stage 1 book.

Key background information
Graphic notation is one of the most accessible and flexible forms of notation. It involves thinking up and writing down an abstract symbol to represent either a sound that you wish to make, or a sound that is already in the composition. It can be used to record a child's complex composition that is already composed, or to create an instant composition that can be read and interpreted differently by everyone who plays it. It can take a variety of forms and be laid out in many two-dimensional or even three-dimensional shapes.

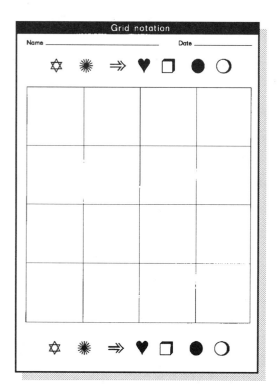

Moving forward
'Jumped up Mozart' on page 59 uses the grid method both for notation and as a composing tool. Any compositions that the children make could be notated using this grid.

Notation

In Western classical music, graphic notation has been used by the avant-garde movement and a range of contemporary composers as a means of notating full scale concert pieces. Often the reason for this was to increase the artistic influence of each individual player, and also to enable the composer to write down music to be played on a washing machine, vacuum cleaner or motor bike. Graphic notation also offers children the freedom to experiment with 'found instruments' as well as recording their own compositions on more familiar instruments (see 'Something for nothing' in the *Using instruments* chapter of the Key Stage 1 book).

In terms of primary music, graphic notation offers a structured way of dealing with composition. It allows children to be free and as imaginative and creative as they wish, yet it gives them something concrete to follow. This activity is written assuming the children have composed a piece that they wish to notate. If it is the first time you are doing this activity, have the whole class notating the same piece of music. A composition by the whole class would work well (use activities from the *Composing* chapter) or use one group's composition.

Vocabulary

Symbol, abstract, representation, imagination, graphic notation.

Preparation

Decide what form you wish the notation to take – a spiral, a long thin strip, a cube, written on A3 paper – and prepare the materials accordingly. Assemble a selection of pencils, felt-tipped pens or paint depending on which medium you prefer to work with. Collect a wide selection of instruments if you wish to work with them – the activity can work with instruments, body percussion or a mixture of both (remember to give opportunities to all the children to play the instruments). Either pin up a large piece of paper or use a white board. Sheet 127 could be used for this activity.

Resources needed

White board or large piece of paper, felt-tipped pens, pencils or paint, instruments, materials, blank cassette tape and cassette player if required.

What to do

Seat all the children where they can see you and the paper. Draw a simple coloured symbol or squiggle on the paper – make it obviously either a sharp or smooth, loud or quiet symbol. Without saying anything draw three more symbols that are contrasting both with each other and the first one. Making sure the children are watching, get out the instruments that you have collected and lay them out in front of them. Stand quietly for a second, the children will either be on tenterhooks or desperately calling out/putting up their hands to say 'Miss can I play the drum?' and so on. Ignore all interruptions and point out the first symbol – ask them what type of sound they think should be played for it. Should it be a loud or soft sound, high or low, scary, exciting, jumpy, spiky, long or short, sweet, lingering? When they have thought about this ask them which instrument should be used and what you should do with it. If you are using body percussion, you will have to go straight into asking the above questions without any mention of instrument choices.

As they decide on the sounds, give out the chosen instruments to specific children; ask them to stand up and play the required sound as you point to each symbol in turn. (If you are using body percussion, do the same for each clap, stamp and so on.)

After this initial performance, add to the composition by repeating a few symbols several times. Ask the same children to perform this piece, pointing to each symbol in the same way as before. When this is over, ask the children how they could show on the paper one of the instruments or sounds playing continuously throughout the piece, while other sounds are played occasionally. The children will probably suggest a variety of things: continuing the line from the original symbol, shading in the colour of the symbol, writing in words. (All these suggestions would be fine, although writing is not really graphic notation.) Then ask them what you should do when you get to the end of the line on your paper. Take up the suggestions that you find most suitable and draw them onto the paper. Play the revised piece and ask the children's opinion. What did they think of the length, the combination of instruments, the beginning, the end? Ask them if they found the notation easy to follow and, if not, what were the problems and how might they be solved. How could they improve the music or the notation?

If they seem to be pleased about the work, tell them they are going to have the opportunity to try exactly the same thing as you have just done. Put the children into groups of four or five. Explain that they must draw a series of symbols to represent a series of different sounds, some of which will be continued while other instruments or sounds are only made occasionally. Remind them of the need to have a good start and a good finish.

Give the children five to seven minutes to finish and practise their piece before you ask each group to give a performance. This would be a good opportunity to record the music.

Suggestion(s) for extension

If the children are finding the activity easy, ask them to add two more colours so that more symbols can be notated and played. Ask them to make up a tune with a particular mood – it could be a sad, puzzled or happy one.

Suggestion(s) for support

If some children find this activity difficult it will probably be because they are unable to follow the notation quickly enough. Go over the work and play the music again, this time using just three symbols and leaving plenty of time so that the children are not feeling hurried.

Assessment opportunities

This activity provides opportunities to assess whether a child can follow simple notation and whether they can represent a sound with a symbol.

Opportunities for IT

The children could work in groups and use a drawing program to reproduce their initial notation. They could create simple shapes and pictures, sometimes called stamps, which they can place, copy and move around within the picture to give ideas of repeating patterns of shapes and sounds. The children could work in different shades or patterns of the same colour depending on the mood of the music. Each group's work could be printed out and bound together to make a class book of notations.

Display ideas

The graphic notation sheets the children design make a lovely display. Accompany these with a brief explanation by the children of what they were doing and how they were doing it together with recordings of their performances.

Moving forward

Repeat the activity as many times as you wish using topic work as inspiration, with the children notating their own compositions. This activity links to 'Journey line' on page 44. 'Listening collage' on page 48 is an activity that uses graphic notation in a more advanced way.

BEAT SUMS AND BAR LINES

To introduce the principle of time value (the lengths of notes) in formal notation.

✝✝ *Session one: whole class and individuals or pairs.*
Session two: individuals or pairs.

🕐 *Two 45-minute sessions.*

🎵 *Medium.*

Previous skills/knowledge needed

The children need to understand the idea of a steady pulse: 'Copy and echo' on page 19 would be useful for this. They also need to be able to count in sets of beats: 'Stars in your eyes' in this chapter provides useful experience here.

Key background information

This activity is designed to introduce you and the children to some of the basic principles of *formal* or *stave* (staff) notation. This 'Western' notation is quite unusual. In many musical traditions notation is not used at all – the West are really the odd ones out!

In particular, the activity focuses on *time value* – the way note-lengths are represented – and the division of a piece of music into sets of beats, called *bars*. The activity will help children to make sense of formal notation when they see it and enable them to use elements of it to represent rhythms in their own compositions. It draws on their experience, gained through other activities, of feeling a beat, learning rhythmic patterns and counting in sets of three or four.

The activity introduces the basic vocabulary of note-lengths: *crotchet* (the type of note used here for one beat), *minim* (two-beat note), *semibreve* (four-beat note) and *quaver* (half-beat note). Different approaches use different terminology for these note-lengths; do not worry if you see a crotchet referred to as a 'quarter-note' for example. This

term is based on the fact that all the note-values are divisions of the semibreve, which is a 'whole note'. The reason the crotchet as a one-beat note is focused on here rather than as a part of a semibreve, is that it helps children to think and count in sets of beats, with the unit (the crotchet) most commonly used as a single beat.

Vocabulary
Beat, bar, set, crotchet, minim, semibreve, quaver, formal notation, stave.

Preparation
Draw the two diagrams below onto the white board or a large sheet of paper on a flip chart.

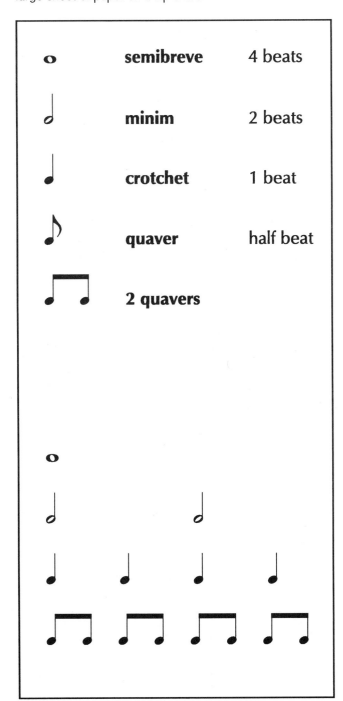

Remind yourself of the time-value of each type of note (semibreve = 4 beats, and so on) and practise clapping through the pattern of beats in the second diagram – which will sound like this (* means one clap):

1	2	3	4
*			
1	2	3	4
*		*	
1	2	3	4
*	*	*	*
1	2	3	4
* *	* *	* *	* *

Resources needed
Marker pens, white board/flip chart, one copy of photocopiable sheets 144 and 145 for each child or pair, writing materials.

What to do
Session one
Tell the children that they are going to learn how to recognise notes of different lengths using (Western) formal notation. Show them the first diagram on the board and explain the time value of each type of note, starting with the crotchet (the one-beat note). Now set up a steady count of 1 – 2 – 3 – 4 – 1 – 2 – 3 – 4 and clap through the second diagram with them, counting all the time as you clap. Ask them if they can hear how many crotchets fit into four beats, how many quavers and so on.

Now tell the children that they are going to do some 'beat sums'. Give out photocopiable sheet 144 and ask them to work out (either individually or in pairs) how many beats each sum adds up to. For your convenience, the answers to the sums are given below in the 'Reference to photocopiable sheets'. When the children have completed the sums, ask them to work in pairs and try clapping the rhythm of each line, keeping a steady pulse of 1– 2 – 3 – 4 throughout.

When the pairs have had a chance to try this, clap through the patterns with the whole class, keeping up a count of 1– 2 – 3 – 4 as above. Ask the children if they have noticed that all the patterns are in sets of four beats. Go through the answers to the beat sums and point out that every answer is a multiple of four, reminding the children of the sets of four beats they heard when they were clapping the rhythm. Tell them that almost all the tunes they know will be organised into sets of either three or four beats. Let them try singing or humming a few of the songs they know to demonstrate this, then ask if anyone can think of a children's song which begins with the pattern of beat sum number 10. Suggest 'This Old Man' (unless someone already has) and ask the children to sing 'This old man, he played one', clapping the pattern as they sing. Conclude this session by singing 'This Old Man' all the way through, clapping the rhythm.

Notation

Session two

Begin the session by reminding the children of the beat sums they did in session one, and of the way that the rhythm of beat sum number 10 was the same as the first phrase of 'This Old Man'. Give out a copy of photocopiable sheet 145 to each child or pair and point out that the tune on the sheet has not yet been split into sets of beats (or *bars*), but that the 4/4 figure at the beginning of the tune shows that each bar should contain four crotchet beats. Tell them that the set of five lines on which the notes are written is called a *stave* and that sometimes, music written like this is called *stave notation*.

Sing through the song once or twice asking the children to point to the notes on the sheet as they sing. Ask them to tell you where the end of the first set of four beats comes. They should be able to tell you that it is after the first ♩ ♩ ♩ pattern. Ask them to draw a *bar line*, a vertical line from the top to the bottom of the stave, after this pattern (demonstrate on the board if necessary). Now ask them to count on in sets of four beats through the whole song, working individually or in pairs, drawing in a bar line after each set.

Check through the bar lines with the whole class, reminding them that you are counting in sets of four beats all the way through the song. Their finished results should look like the illustration below. Conclude the session by asking the class to sing through the song again, this time just clapping on the *first* beat of every bar, so that the idea of sets of beats (bars) is reinforced.

Suggestion(s) for extension

Children who have taken well to this activity can try playing 'This Old Man' on xylophones or keyboards (the note-names are marked under the tune on the photocopiable sheet). If they do this in groups, one or two children can play the tune while the rest of the group play the first beat of each bar on percussion instruments.

Suggestion(s) for support

Some children will find it hard to grasp the concept of sets of beats (bars). It will help if you go through the song with them, clapping your hands or tapping on their shoulders on the first of every four beats.

Assessment opportunities

This activity enables you to monitor the children's understanding of time value in formal notation, and their ability to split a piece of simple written music into its component bars (sets of beats).

Opportunities for IT

The children could use a simple software notation program, such as *Notate,* to generate their own beat sums or rhythmic patterns for each other to try. It is worth remembering that all Acorn RISCOS computers are supplied with a simple notation package called *Maestro* which could be used for this work.

The teacher could also set up a keyboard linked to the computer through a MIDI interface with notation software, so that the children can experiment with different rhythms played on the keyboard and see how the software automatically notates their work.

Display ideas

You or the children could write out some well-known tunes on enlarged staves with the bar lines missing. Moveable bar lines could be made out of black card or plastic for the children to attach to the staves, using Blu-Tack or drawing pins. A chart showing the time-values of the notes (as in the diagram on page 111) could be displayed alongside the songs. The

children could also make recordings of the songs, using percussion to emphasise the first beat of each bar, and add these to the display.

Reference to photocopiable sheets

Photocopiable sheet 144 contains a set of 'beat sums' to which the following answers correspond: 1) 16, 2) 8, 3) 4, 4) 8, 5) 8, 6) 8, 7) 8, 8) 4, 9) 8, 10) 8. Photocopiable sheet 145

is a score of 'This Old Man', showing the notes and their names, but with no bar lines.

Moving forward

The focus on sets of beats in this activity links well with 'African polyrhythms' on page 80, which explores unusual combinations of beats. You can also repeat this activity any number of times, making up your own beat sums, and using tunes from song books with the bar lines deleted for the children to replace.

CHOPPING UP A SONG

To introduce the principle of pitch notation (writing down notes on a stave), and to develop awareness of the way in which musical phrases can be combined to make a tune.

†† *Whole class, then groups of three or four.*

⏰ *60 minutes.*

♫ *Advanced.*

Previous skills/knowledge needed

This activity follows on directly from 'Beat sums and bar lines' in this chapter, using the same song ('This Old Man') and building on the children's familiarity with the tune. If you are not intending to do the above activity first, follow the instructions in 'Preparation'. The children will need to be able to sing 'This Old Man' confidently for this activity. It will also help if they are familiar with playing tuned percussion (xylophones, for example), though this is not essential.

Key background information

The aim of this activity is to enable children to see how a tune is written down as a series of notes on a stave – this is the aspect of formal notation known as *pitch notation*. This is demonstrated first by looking at and singing the song in its usual form, then by rearranging parts of it so that the tune is altered. The intention is not to teach pitch notation directly, but to help children to understand how it works by encouraging them to *see* different patterns of notes on the stave, and *hear* the musical phrases they represent. As well as making new tunes from the components of the original one, the children will be able to hear how some phrases

sound 'wrong' in certain positions. (Try starting the tune with the notes that go with 'This old man came rolling home', for example, and see whether it sounds right.) They will, therefore, have an opportunity to find which combinations of phrases 'work well' and which do not. The activity helps to develop the children's compositional skills as well as their awareness of formal notation.

Vocabulary

Note, bar, phrase, tune, melody, pitch notation, formal notation.

Preparation

If you have already done 'Beat sums and bar lines', you need to get out the children's photocopiable sheet 145 with the bar lines drawn onto them. If not, draw the bar lines onto one copy of the sheet (see the activity for an illustration of where they go) and make one copy of the altered sheet for each child. You also need to enlarge one copy of the completed sheet onto A3 and make a pointer for conducting: a long roll of paper with a point at the end works well. If you would like the children to evaluate their composition or performance, make a copy of sheets 151 or 154 and 155 for each child as necessary.

Resources needed

One completed copy of photocopiable sheet 145 for each child (see 'Preparation'), an enlarged A3 version, a pointer, a pair of scissors for each group, one instrument with note-names marked on it for each group (for example, xylophones, glockenspiels, sets of chime bars containing the notes C D E F G A), copies of sheets 151, 154 and 155 if required.

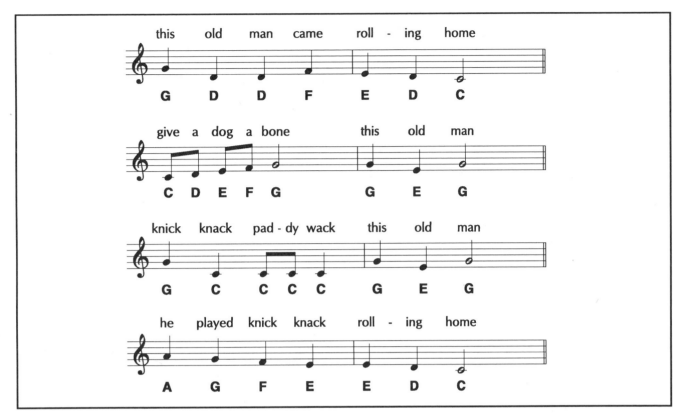

What to do

Show the children the enlarged copy of photocopiable sheet 145 and ask for a volunteer to come and conduct the song by pointing to the *notes* (not the words) as the rest of the class sings. Repeat this a couple of times with different conductors, then ask the next conductor to try and trick the class by starting somewhere other than the beginning of the song and pointing to *four* bars at random. (The conductor can choose the same bar more than once if he or she likes.) The children following the conductor might find themselves singing something like the two examples above.

By selecting just four bars at a time, the children can hear the overall shape of the tunes they have made. After they have tried two or three different tunes with different conductors, try asking them whether each new tune (or *melody*) has a good beginning and a good ending, and whether the second set of two bars (or the second *phrase*) makes a good answer to the first set.

Now divide the class into groups of three or four and give out a copy of sheet 145 to each child, and a pair of scissors and an instrument to each group. The task for each group is to compose a number of four-bar melodies by cutting up and rearranging the bars of the song on their sheet. Suggest that they start by cutting up just one sheet then add bars from the others as and when they need them. They can use any of the bars more than once if they like. Tell them to try out their tunes using the instruments provided (as well as singing the words if they like), and to continue to rearrange the bars of each short composition until the group is satisfied with it. Give the groups about 20 minutes to work, then bring

them back together and ask each one to perform their tunes to the rest of the class. Ask the groups to introduce each tune with an explanation of the decisions they made that lead them to their final version. Ask the children to evaluate each others' work, commenting on beginnings and endings, and the way in which the phrases they have chosen contrast with or answer each other. As a follow-up, you might like to use the evaluative sheets 151, 154 and 155 which invite the children to reflect on their compositions and performance.

Suggestion(s) for extension

Children who manage this activity well can be asked to add either *harmonies* (additional notes which go together well with the ones they have chosen) or *rhythmic accompaniments* (for example, using untuned percussion) to their group compositions. They could try creating longer composition, using eight bars instead of four. You could also ask these children to identify the crotchets, quavers, minims and semibreves in 'This Old Man' and their own tunes, referring back to the activity 'Beat sums and bar lines' in this chapter.

Suggestion(s) for support

Some children will find it difficult to remember how the different parts of the tune go when they are arranged in a different order. It will help if you ask them to work alongside someone who is more confident. You can also make them the instrument player for their group; this will give them an important role in their group which will have the effect of increasing their self-confidence.

Notation

Reference to photocopiable sheets

Photocopiable sheet 145 shows the words, tune and note-names of 'This Old Man', which the children can rearrange and play or sing. Photocopiable sheet 151 invites children to evaluate their own composition, while photocopiable sheets 154 and 155 invite them to evaluate their own performance.

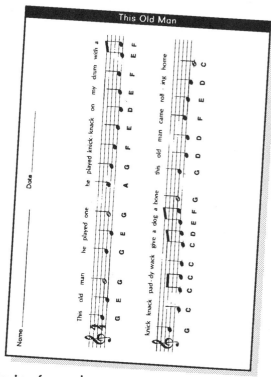

Assessment opportunities

This activity will enable you to monitor children's understanding of the principle of pitch notation, and their ability to select and combine musical phrases to make a tune. It also shows how capable they are of evaluating their own and each others' compositions.

Opportunities for IT

They could use software such as *Compose World* that uses set phrases which the children can arrange to create a tune. They can try out the different phrases in a number of ways and look at the structure of the tune as well.

The children could also use a keyboard linked to the computer using a MIDI interface and running notation software, such as *Rhapsody*. They can experiment with different tune sequences played on the keyboard and see how the software automatically notates their work. They can then play back their work using either just the computer or the sound facilities of the keyboard. The children can follow the sounds in relation to the notation they have created and see how the pattern of notes on the stave matches the tunes created.

Display ideas

Each group can stick their compositions onto paper or card and display them alongside the original song. They can map each bar of their compositions onto the original tune by joining them with a line or thread. Recordings of both the original song and the group compositions could be made available next to the display.

Moving forward

The more often you repeat this activity, the more extended and complex the children's compositions will become, and the more comfortable they will feel with formal notation. For example, they might want to include repeated sections (sets of bars), or create two different tunes and combine them into an A – B – A structure. It is a good idea to suggest that they always work in multiples of four bars, as this will give their pieces a discernible structure. The children can also move on to notating their own compositions, using the knowledge they have gained here.

Assessment

Our rationale for assessment at Key Stage 2 is the same as that for Key Stage 1: it happens all the time (whether it is written down or not), every activity is an assessment activity, and assessment is primarily about noticing what children are doing and deciding where to go next. In this chapter these ideas are explored a little further, and a range of practical recording formats are provided for you to use or adapt as you wish. Specialists will continue to argue about whether and how music should be assessed for years to come. This book does not pretend to resolve that argument, but offers some down-to-earth suggestions as to how you can make the most of what you notice – and gather some useful evidence for OFSTED inspections into the bargain.

ASSESSMENT IN MUSIC

Many teachers worry more about assessing music than about teaching it. You may feel that musical learning is so hard to pin down that it is impossible to define. Or you may think, especially if you are a non-specialist, that you could not possibly attempt to make a judgement on the children's progress as you have so little musical experience yourself. Whatever your feelings about assessment, you may be constantly frustrated by the fact that the musical skills and understanding the children display one week may seem to have evaporated by the next! It will help if you think of assessment not as a *test* to determine exactly what levels the children have reached, but as a *guide* to suggest how you might respond to them and where you might go next. In view of this there are *three points* that need to be made.

1. Assessment in music happens all the time.

You do not need to do extra assessment activities to find out what the children have learned. All the activities in this book are assessment activities, and every time you notice something a child is doing in music, you are carrying out assessment. The points that are most likely to emerge are listed in the 'Assessment opportunities' at the end of each activity, but be on the lookout for the unexpected. Children with special needs, for example, will often shine in music when they find it hard to achieve in other areas.

2. Assessment does not have to be written down.

Assessment should not be confused with recording; most of the assessment you carry out will simply consist of noticing and responding to what the children are doing. However, it may be useful to keep a record of the most significant factors, to help when you need to report to parents, other teachers and the children themselves on their progress. Four possible ways of recording this information to suit different teacher's styles and preferences are shown below (see 'Recording sheets'), or you may prefer to devise your own.

3. There is no National Curriculum requirement for formal assessment in music.

There are no primary music SATs, and teachers' own assessments are not reviewed by external moderators. However, you *are* required to make yearly reports to parents, and to undertake a summary assessment at the end of each Key Stage, based on the end of Key Stage Statements in the National Curriculum document. This is made much easier (especially for the harassed Year 6 teacher!) if a brief musical profile is built up gradually throughout the Key Stage. If a series of 'snapshots' has been compiled over the years, you should have a useful general picture of the child's musical development by the end of Year 6. Records of this sort will also provide you with the kind of evidence OFSTED want to see of musical progression taking place through a range of experiences, supported by a useful and usable assessment and recording system. You might also collect recordings of the children's work, photographs, videos, pictures and evidence of what the children say or write about their work in music, to show which musical activities have taken place and the effect they have had.

Recording sheets

These sheets can be used in conjunction with most of the activities in this book. They present the learning outcomes covered by the National Curriculum using everyday language in a range of different formats. Some formats offer a lot of detail while others suggest general headings under which you can make your own observations. If you find that none of these formats suit you, you may prefer to use the wording of the National Curriculum document itself.

Assessment grid (pages 146 and 147)

This is a summary of all the points raised in 'Assessment opportunities' throughout the book. The points are grouped in the grid (which takes up two pages) to show how they relate to each other, but you will find that each activity in the book addresses a whole range of items on the list. You can use the photocopiable sheets as a checklist to provide an at-a-glance record for the whole class. This might be updated termly or half-yearly, to reflect the developing skills of the children and to show which areas might need more attention.

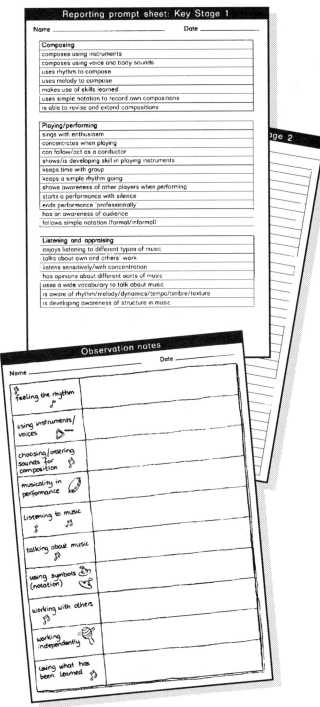

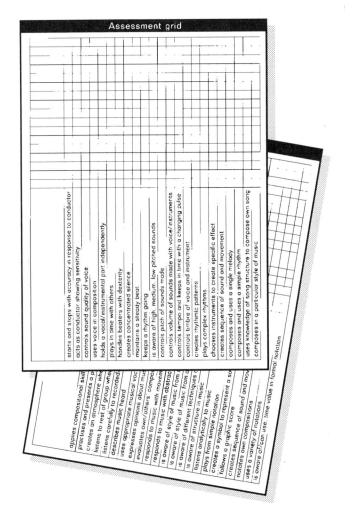

Reporting prompt sheets (pages 148 and 149)

These sheets outline the kinds of comments you might make about the children's progress, grouped under the National Curriculum headings. Sheets for both Key Stage 1 and Key

Stage 2 are included, as some children may still have had very little musical experience by the beginning of Key Stage 2. Remember that the Key Stage 2 comments should serve you right up to the end of Year 6.

Observation notes (page 150)

This is an open-ended assessment and recording sheet, which suggests ten ways in which you might see children developing musically. You can either use one sheet for each child, building up an individual musical profile throughout their primary years, or start a new sheet for each child every year. A similar sheet is used in the Key Stage 1 book, to allow for continuity from one Key Stage to another.

Self-assessment sheets (pages 151 to 157)

These are for the children to use on their own, or with a little help from you. 'Evaluate your composing skills' page 151 and 'We are the greatest' page 152 invite children to evaluate single compositions and performances respectively, and can be used any number of times throughout the key stage. 'Music notes' page 152 and 'Are you a star?' pages 154 and 155, invite children to reflect on their composing and performing progress at the end of the term or year. 'Are you all ears?' page 156 is designed as a cumulative record of listening skills in Years 3 and 4, to be followed by 'How well do you listen?' page 157 in Years 5 and 6. All these sheets can be kept as evidence of the children's musical progression, along with other examples of their work. Opportunities arise throughout the book for children to use these self-assessment sheets within different activities.

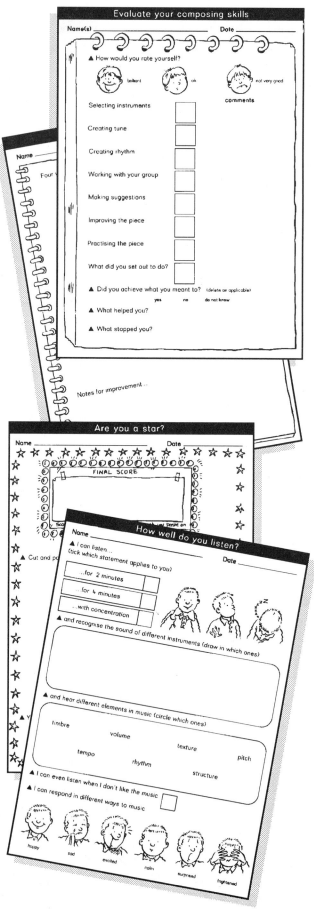

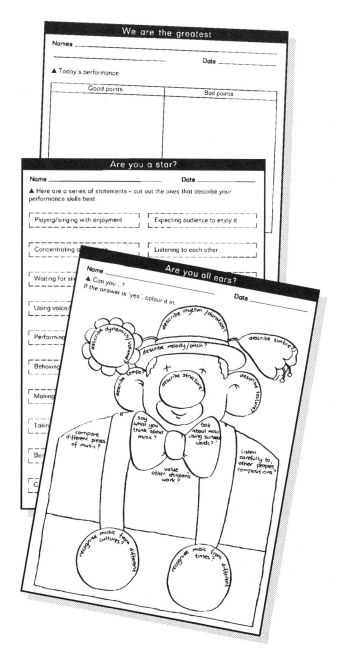

Photocopiables

The pages in this section can be photocopied for use in the classroom or school which has purchased this book, and do not need to be declared in any return in respect of any photocopying licence.

They comprise a varied selection of both pupil and teacher resources, including pupil worksheets, resource material and record sheets to be completed by the teacher or children. Most of the photocopiable pages are related to individual activities in the book; the name of the activity is indicated at the top of the sheet, together with a page reference indicating where the lesson plan for that activity can be found.

Individual pages are discussed in detail within each lesson plan, accompanied by ideas for adaptation where appropriate – of course, each sheet can be adapted to suit your own needs and those of your class. Sheets can also be coloured, laminated, mounted on to card, enlarged and so on where appropriate.

Pupil worksheets and record sheets have spaces provided for children's names and for noting the date on which each sheet was used. This means that, if so required, they can be included easily within any pupil assessment portfolio.

(See pages 14, 17 and 18)

The language of conducting

There are numerous ways in which you can signal to children to start, stop, get louder, get quieter, join in, fade out and so on. You may already be perfectly comfortable with your own set of signals. The suggestions made here are just to guide you on your way if the whole idea of conducting is new to you. (Do not forget that the children need to learn to conduct each other too – they should be doing this with even the simplest of activities.) Feel free to try out a range of possibilities: you may find that one signal suits you better than another. As you and the children become more adept at using and following signals, you can try conducting one group with one hand and another group with the other.

Bringing in individuals
hand gesture or nod or eyes

Stop
closed fist or bring finger and thumb/hands together

Holding a long note
finger and thumb apart, moving slowly in a parallel line until closed to stop

I sing/play
point to self

Loud
hands wide apart or eyes wide

Getting louder
hands increasingly far apart or eyes increasingly wide

High part
flat outstretched hand held high or point upwards

Gently
hands outstretched, palms to floor, with rocking movement

Bringing in groups
hands parallel or vertical downwards hand movement, inviting group to start

Keep going
'cranking handle' motion with arm or hands outstretched to receive

You sing/play
point to others

Quiet
finger to lips or hands/fingers close together

Getting quieter
hands/fingers increasingly close together

Low part
outstretched hand held low or point downwards

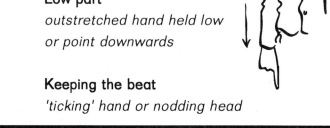

Keeping the beat
'ticking' hand or nodding head

MUSIC

(See page 25)

Ideas for responding to children's compositions

Try using these as a starting point for responding to what children have done.

'I like the way you...'

▲ had the instruments starting/finishing together/one by one;

▲ showed contrast in the piece (loud/quiet; high/low; fast/slow; sound/silence);

▲ chose/used instruments carefully to suit the atmosphere you were creating;

▲ built up to a climax/died away to nothing;

▲ used the loud instruments to make it dramatic/scary/majestic;

▲ used the quiet instruments to make it eerie/sad/gentle;

▲ used the single note on the triangle/chime bar/drum to create an effect;

▲ repeated the beginning/middle/end section of the piece;

▲ repeated the third/fourth/fifth note/tune/rhythm;

▲ changed the rhythm/tune/beginning/middle/end when you repeated it;

▲ worked independently/worked together as a group/shared ideas;

▲ used the rhythm/tune from... as part of your piece;

▲ remembered what you had composed before and incorporated it here.

'Can you tell us...'

▲ what kind of effect you were aiming to create?

▲ which part you wanted to be the loudest/quietest/happiest/most dramatic?

▲ what made you choose the drum/cymbal/xylophone?

▲ how you decided which instruments to use?

▲ how you decided what to play on each instrument?

▲ whether it sounded the way you wanted when you played it to us?

(See page 25)

Ideas for extending children's compositions

Try making these suggestions to the children.

'Why don't you...'
▲ repeat the whole piece two/three/four times;

▲ repeat the melody two/three/four times with different instruments playing the rhythm;

▲ play the whole piece once loudly, then once quietly;

▲ have two children playing the rhythm/tune together on different instruments;

▲ put in a pause/a silence/a surprise;

▲ get louder/softer/faster/slower for the ending;

▲ start/finish one by one;

▲ start/finish all together with a crash/with a long note/with a sudden stop;

▲ add harmonies to the tune (that is, notes that sound good together);

▲ add a second tune to follow the first;

▲ add extra rhythms that fit together.

Diced sounds (see page 26)

Diced sounds

Players _____   Date _____

Rhythm	Tune

Roman sound picture (see page 28)

Roman building

Name(s) _____   Date _____

Job allocated –
These are the sounds of the job:

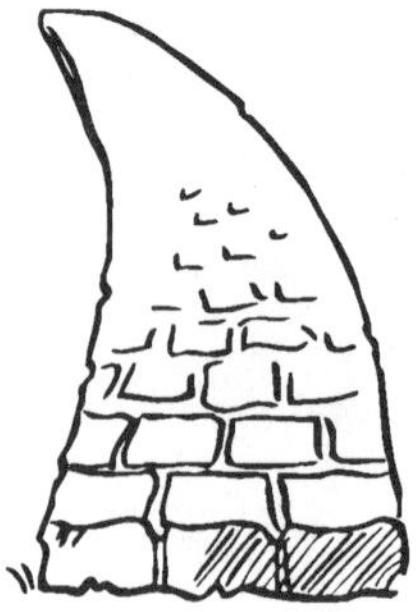

Instruments chosen for composition
Instrument   Sounds they represent

What do you think of it?

What did other people say?

Any improvements you want to make to the composition?

Signed _____

Pavement café (see page 31) and Graphic notation – instant composition (see page 108)

Graphic score

Composition Title _____

Composed by _____

_____ Date _____

Performance poetry (see page 34)

What a performance!

Play No Ball

What a wall!
Play No ball,
It tells us all.
Play No Ball,
  By Order!

Lick no lolly.
Skip no rope.
Nurse no dolly.
Wish no hope.
Hop no scotch.
Ring no bell.
Telly no watch.
Joke no tell.
Fight no friend.
Up no make.
Penny no lend.
Hand no shake.
Tyre no pump.
Down no fall.
Up no jump.
Name no call.
  And...
Play No Ball.
No Ball. No Ball.
  BY ORDER!

Gerard Benson

Gerard Benson (1992) *The Magnificent Callisto*, Blackie Children's Books. Penguin. ISBN 0-216-93267-X

Talking about music (see page 40)

Music talk

Name _____   Date _____

Music listened to _____

▲ Musical vocabulary

thunderous

slow

sweet

clear

jumping

spooky

sad

sliding

atmospheric

fast

happy

soppy

flowing

frightening

Talking about music (see page 40)

Timbre vocabulary

Name _____   Date _____

Music listened to _____

▲ Timbre words

hard

dull

cold

soft tinny

booming

warm

ringing

resounding

echoey echoey
echoey echoey
echoey
echoey

jingling

bright

piercing

Talking about music (see page 40)

Texture vocabulary

Name _____ Date _____

Music heard _____ by _____

▲ Texture words

smooth busy undulating

duet quiet spiky

rough

solo ╪ stark silky

crunchy

blending blending blending

thin velvety

tangle

orchestral empty

Chunky lumpy

Talking about music (see page 40)

What do *you* think is happening?

Name _____   Date _____

▲ Jot down some ideas in words and sketches in the bubbles below.

Talking about music (see page 40)

Musical comparisons

Name(s) _____   Date _____

You can compare music in lots of different ways. Here are some suggestions – underline the ones you are using.

▲ List the similarities and differences.

▲ Write what you notice about each piece of music.

▲ Think of some words to describe each piece of music (write them down too!).

▲ Explain how each composer creates moods and effects.

Title _____

by _____

Title _____

by _____

Talking about music (see page 40)

How do they do that?

Name _____ Date _____

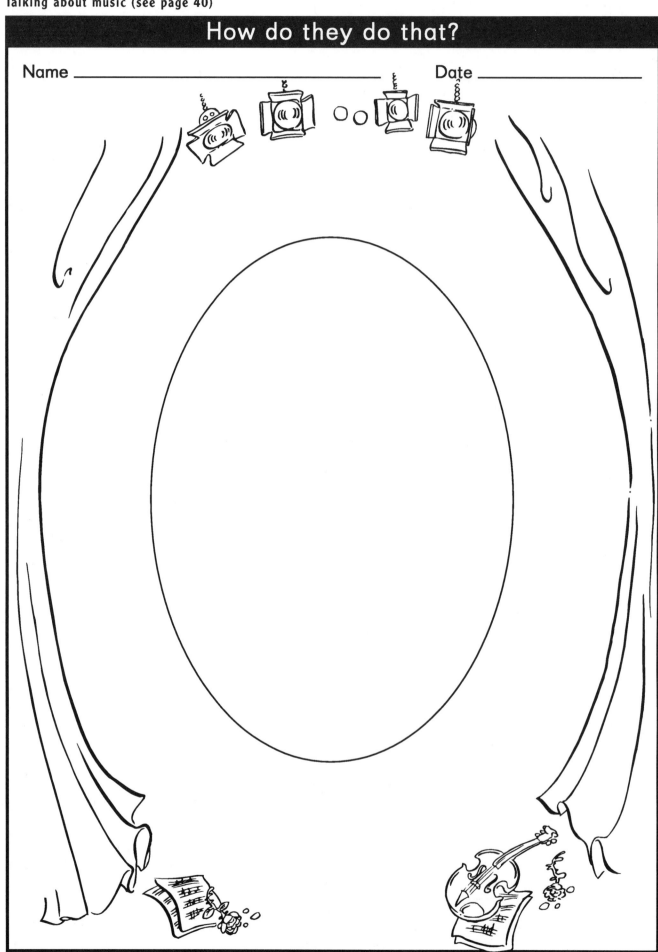

Talking about music (see page 40)

Responding to music

Name of listener_____ Date _____

Title of music _____

Which part did you like the best?

Which part did you find most interesting?

What did you think of the beginning/end?

What instruments did you hear?

How were they used?

What atmosphere was portrayed?

If you were writing this music what would you do differently?

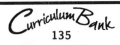

Talking about music (see page 40)

Music review

Name _____   Date _____

This week's Music Review is _____

by _____ written in the year _____

My first impression

The above photograph is of...

When I think more about it

Focusing on composing

Focusing on performance

Reviewer's tips for improving the composition

Reviewer's rating

ok/I'm still thinking

enjoyed it/good

didn't like it at all

Tudor pastimes (see page 52)

Royal Consort of Musicians

Name(s) _____   Date _____

▲ List your instruments and players here and show what rhythms or notes you play.

hurdy-gurdy

trombone

sackbut

lute

Basic baroque (see page 56)

Brandenburg Concerto No 2 by J S Bach

Name _____

Date _____

	Start	15 seconds	30 seconds	45 seconds	1 minute	1 minute 15 seconds	1 minute 30 seconds
Trumpet							
Recorder							
Oboe							
Solo Violin							
Violin Ensemble							
Harpsichord							
Cello							

Telling tales: music for ballet (see page 62)

Ballet commission

Name _____   Date _____

▲ You have been commissioned to write a ballet score. You are free to choose any well-known story and any combination of instrumental, electronic or vocal sounds you wish. Think carefully about what story you would choose and how you would use music to represent the characters and events in the story. Describe your choices below.

▲ The story we have chosen for our ballet is:_____

We will use these instruments and sounds to tell the story

Waltzing Victorians (see page 65)

Victorian waltzes

TUNE Whistles recorders	Start on C or E or G	choose from C D E F G A B		end on C or E or G
CHORDS xylophones 'cellos glockenspiels	G G < < C E E	G G < < C E E	G G < < C E E	G G < < C E E
TUNE	Start on C or E or D	choose from C D E F G A B		end on G or B or D
CHORDS	D D < < G B B	D D < < G B B	D D < < G B B	D D < < G B B
TUNE	Start on C or E or G	choose from C D E F G A B		end on C or E or G

CHORDS	G G
	< <
	C E E
		G G
		< <
		C E E
			✢ F< C
			     A G G
			< <
			C E E
				✢ F< C
				     A G G
				< <
				C E E

TUNE	Start on C or E or D	choose from C D E F G A B		end on C or E or G
CHORDS	D D < < G B B	D D < < G B B	G G < < C E E	G E < play all at C the same time here
	um pa pa	um pa pa	um pa pa	um pa pa

This Waltz first performed on _____ by _____

_____ is called _____

Zein's tune (see page 74)

Drumming practice sheet

▲ Repeat each pattern as many times as you wish.

Pattern one
Ta Ticka Ticka Ta, Ta Ticka Ticka Ta

Pattern two
Ticka Ta Ticka Ta, Ta Ta Ticka Ta

Pattern three
Ta Ta Ta Ticka, Ta Ta Ta Ticka

Pattern four
Ta Ticka Ta Ta, Ta Ticka Ta Ta

Pattern five
Ta Ta Ticka Ticka, Ta Ta Ticka Ticka

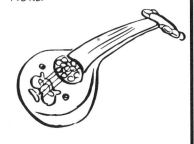

Pattern six – Make up your own...

Recreating a raga (see page 86) and Pattern tracking (see page 96)

Pattern tracking

Name(s)

Date

Pattern tracking: analysing the structure of

Jumped up Mozart (see page 59) and Stars in your eyes (see page 106)

Grid notation

Name _____   Date _____

✡ ✴ ⇒ ♥ ◻ ● ○

✡ ✴ ⇒ ♥ ◻ ● ○

Beat sums and bar lines (see page 110)

Beat sums

Name _____ Date _____

How many beats in each sum?

▲ Add them up and write the total, then clap the patterns.

1. o + o + o + o = ☐

2. ♩ + ♩ + ♩ + ♩ = ☐

3. ♫ + ♩ + ♩ = ☐

4. ♩ + ♩ + ♫ + ♫ + ♩ + ♩ = ☐

5. ♩ + ♩ + ♩ + o = ☐

6. ♩ + ♫ + ♫ + ♩ + ♩ = ☐

7. ♩ + ♩ + o = ☐

8. ♫ + ♫ + ♩ + ♩ = ☐

9. ♩ + ♩ + ♫ + ♫ + ♩ = ☐

10. ♩ + ♩ + ♩ + ♩ + ♩ + ♩ = ☐

Beat sums and bar lines (see page 110) and Chopping up a song (see page 114)

This Old Man

Name _____

Date _____

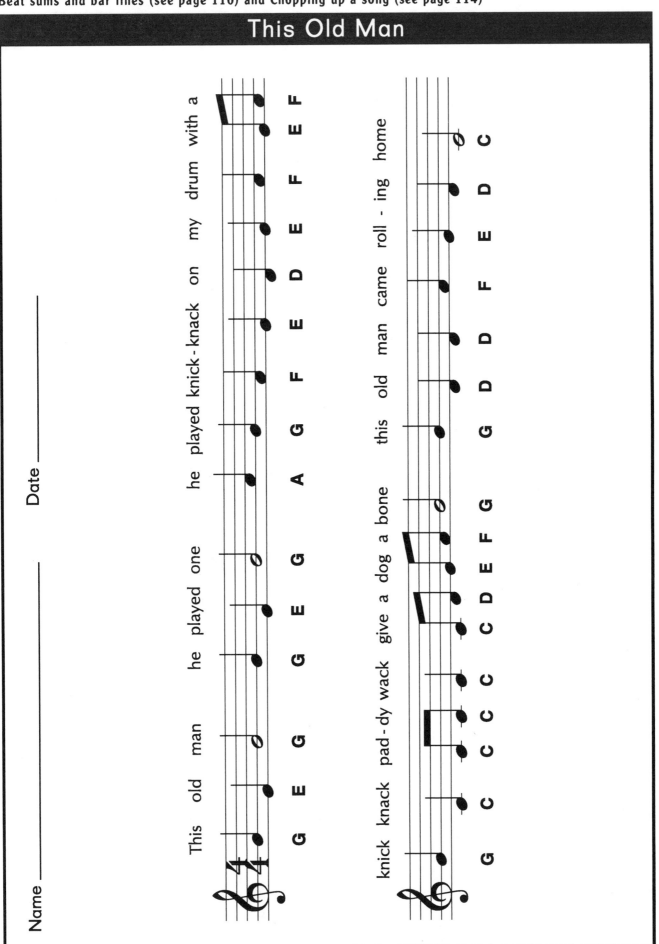

(See page 119)

Assessment grid

	starts and stops with accuracy in response to conductor	acts as conductor showing sensitivity	controls sound quality of voice	uses voice in composition	holds a vocal/instrumental part independently	plays in time with others	handles beaters with dexterity	creates concentrated silence	maintains a steady beat	keeps a rhythm going	is aware of high, medium, low pitched sounds	controls pitch of sounds made	controls volume of sounds made with voice/instruments	controls tempo and keeps in time with a changing pulse	controls timbre of voice and instrument	creates rhythmic patterns	plays complex rhythms	chooses instruments to create specific effect	creates sequence of sound and movement	composes and uses a single melody	composes and uses a simple rhythm	uses knowledge of song structure to compose own song	composes in a particular style of music

(See page 119)

Assessment grid continued

		applies compositional skills learned	practises and presents a performance	creates an atmosphere when performing	listens to rest of group when performing	listens carefully to recorded/own compositions	describes music heard	uses appropriate musical vocabulary in description	expresses opinions about music	evaluates own/others' compositions	responds to music with movement	responds to music with abstract images	is aware of style of music from different places	is aware of style of music from different times	is aware of different techniques creating varying effects	is aware of structure in music	listens analytically to music	plays from simple notation	creates a symbol to represent a sound	follows a graphic score	creates sequence of sound and movement	notates own compositions	uses a variety of notations	is aware of/can use, time value in formal notation

(See page 119)

Reporting prompt sheet: Key Stage 1

Name _____   Date _____

Composing
composes using instruments
composes using voice and body sounds
uses rhythm to compose
uses melody to compose
makes use of skills learned
uses simple notation to record own compositions
is able to revise and extend compositions

Playing/performing
sings with enthusiasm
concentrates when playing
can follow/act as a conductor
shows/is developing skill in playing instruments
keeps time with group
keeps a simple rhythm going
shows awareness of other players when performing
starts a performance with silence
ends performance 'professionally'
has an awareness of audience
follows simple notation (formal/informal)

Listening and appraising
enjoys listening to different types of music
talks about own and others' work
listens sensitively/with concentration
has opinions about different sorts of music
uses a wide vocabulary to talk about music
is aware of rhythm/melody/dynamics/tempo/timbre/texture
is developing awareness of structure in music

(See page 119)

Reporting prompt sheet: Key Stage 2

Name _____   Date _____

Composing
shows rhythmic awareness in composition
uses melody well in composition
uses dynamics/timbre/texture to enhance composition
selects specific sounds to create effect or atmosphere
structures compositions
reworks and develops compositions independently
composes using elements of a chosen style
incorporates other people's music in compositions
applies skills learned to own composition

Playing/performing
acts as/responds to a conductor
singing shows control of pitch/dynamics/phrasing
plays some instruments with confidence
keeps in time with other performers
plays quite complex rhythms/tunes
holds a part while playing/singing
communicates with the rest of the group while performing
starts and ends performances convincingly
draws audience into performance
knows how to practise and refine performance
performs with confidence
follows different forms of notation

Listening and appraising
uses appropriate vocabulary to talk about music
expresses and justifies opinions about music
analyses musical style and structure
is aware of music from different times
is aware of music from different cultures
listens carefully to other people's compositions
values other children's work
is able to compare different pieces of music
describes rhythm/melody/dynamics/tempo/timbre/texture/structure

(See page 119)

Observation notes

Name _____   Date _____

♪ feeling the rhythm ♪	
using instruments/ voices ◁—	
choosing/ordering sounds for composition ♪	
musicality in performance	
listening to music ♪ ♫	
talking about music ♪	
using symbols (notation)	
working with others ♪	
working independently	
using what has been learned ♫	

(See page 120)

Evaluate your composing skills

Name(s) _____   Date _____

▲ How would you rate yourself?

brilliant   ok   not very good

comments

Selecting instruments

Creating tune

Creating rhythm

Working with your group

Making suggestions

Improving the piece

Practising the piece

What did you set out to do?

▲ Did you achieve what you meant to?   (delete as applicable)

yes   no   do not know

▲ What helped you?

▲ What stopped you?

(See page 120)

We are the greatest

Names _____

_____   Date _____

▲ Today's performance

Good points	Bad points

▲ Next time, remember...

MUSIC

(See page 120)

Music notes

Name _____   Date _____

Four ways in which I've got better at composition...

Notes for improvement...

(See page 120)

Are you a star?

Name _____   Date _____

▲ Here are a series of statements – cut out the ones that describe your performance skills best.

Playing/singing with enjoyment	Expecting audience to enjoy it
Concentrating all the time	Listening to each other
Waiting for silence	Communicating with rest of group
Using voice/instrument confidently	Remembering what to do
Performing expressively	Playing in time
Behaving like a performer	Starting well
Making sure you rehearsed enough	Finishing well
Taking performance seriously	Controlling instrument well
Being aware of conductor	Creating real silence
Conducting clearly	Paying attention to details in music

(See page 120)

Are you a star?

Name _____ Date _____

FINAL SCORE

Score 1 point for every statement you paste on

▲ Cut and paste your comments here...

▲ Your ideas for improvement

(See page 120)

Are you all ears?

Name _____   Date _____

▲ Can you...?
If the answer is 'yes', colour it in.

MUSIC

(See page 120)

How well do you listen?

Name _____ **Date** _____

▲ I can listen...
(tick which statement applies to you)

...for 2 minutes	
...for 4 minutes	
...with concentration	

▲ and recognise the sound of different instruments (draw in which ones)

▲ and hear different elements in music (circle which ones)

| timbre | volume | texture | pitch |

| tempo | rhythm | structure |

▲ I can even listen when I don't like the music ☐

▲ I can respond in different ways to music

happy   sad   excited   calm   surprised   frightened

INTEGRATING INFORMATION TECHNOLOGY WITHIN MUSIC

Music is predominantly a practical subject and children need to experiment with sounds, instruments, and their own voices. However, there are many opportunities for teachers to use different forms of information technology to develop children's musical skills as well as contribute to the development of their IT capability.

Main IT focus

The main emphasis for the development of IT capability within these music activities is on communicating information with an emphasis on sound.

Music software

There are already a number of specific packages for music which help children to explore sounds, rhythms, composition and notation, and new titles appear regularly. Teachers need to look closely at these before using them in the classroom to make sure that they develop the ideas used by the school. Some of this software enables children to explore different sounds which are made by the computer. The sounds can be based on instruments (often called 'voices'), or the children can create their own 'voices' by changing the parameters of the sound.

Other software uses pre-set sounds that come with the package. Some packages allow children to select sound phrases and join them together to make their own music. Packages like *Compose World* have a range of pre-programmed sound phrases in different styles. These are represented graphically and children can create their own music by selecting and linking them together on a grid. They can use it to make their own compositions and explore musical patterns. Software such as *Music Box* and *Music Explorer* allow children to select individual notes represented in graphic notation on the screen, and to experiment with pitch and chord structures. Many packages also have a rhythm section where children can set up different rhythms using a range of instruments. These can be added as a background to their pitched compositions.

There are numerous notation packages ranging from the simple to the very complex. Many of them are full notation systems which are inappropriate for younger children. Teachers need to check to see whether they are appropriate at the correct level of complexity.

Recording sounds using the computer

One of the interesting additions to most desktop computers has been the ability to record sounds through a microphone connected to the computer. There are two main ways of achieving this. The simplest, especially for Acorn RISCOS computers, is to use a microphone connected to the printer port using an adapter. This still allows the computer's printer to be plugged in although both cannot be used at the same time. The software provided then allows children to record sound samples which can be saved as a sound file. The waveforms of the samples can also be displayed and with some software it is possible to alter the volume and to save a portion of the recorded sample.

The alternative approach is to use a microphone attached to one of the sockets in the computer's sound card (usually applicable to PCs running Windows software). The sound card will provide software for saving and editing the sound sample as already described.

The files created by both systems can be quite large and when using sound samples in multimedia work it may be necessary to limit the length or the number of samples used in relation to the disk space available.

Keyboards

Most schools now have a range of electronic keyboards which children may use for music work. One possibility for schools is to link the keyboard to the computer using a MIDI interface. This is an adapter which usually fits inside the computer, and which interprets the digital music information passed between keyboard and computer.

Using a MIDI interface allows, for example, music played on the keyboard to be automatically notated as the child plays the keyboard by using a package such as *Junior Sibelius*. This composition can then be re-played from the scored version on the computer through the keyboard's own sound system. The music can be edited and re-notated, saved and printed to create scores for other children to use.

An alternative use of the MIDI interface is to allow the sounds created using music software on the computer to be played back through the keyboard's own music system. This usually gives a far superior sound reproduction than the computer's own music interface, particularly if there is no sound card in the computer.

Multi-media authoring software

This software is a recent addition for most schools but is proving to be a very versatile and powerful medium. It allows different pages or screens of information to be linked together.

The other important feature is the software's ability to handle a range of different information including text, pictures from art and drawing packages, digitised pictures from scanned images and pictures from clip art. The software can also handle sound samples which can be recorded using a microphone linked to the computer (usually through the printer port or the sound card) and special software. Sounds can also be taken from audio CDs or commercial sound collections and, where schools have keyboards and a MIDI interface, they can be taken from the keyboard and saved as a sound file on the computer.

IT links

The grids below relate the activities in this book to specific areas of IT and to relevant software resources. Activities are referenced by page number. (Bold page numbers indicate activities that have expanded IT content.) The software listed in the second grid is a selection of programs generally available to primary schools, and is not intended as a recommended list. The software featured should be available from most good educational software retailers.

AREA OF IT	SOFTWARE	ACTIVITIES (PAGE NOS)					
		CHAPTER 2	CHAPTER 3	CHAPTER 4	CHAPTER 5	CHAPTER 6	CHAPTER 7
Communicating information	Word processor/DTP	34		62	76, 80	92	106
Communicating information	Art package	31	42, 44, 48	56		98	
Communicating information	Drawing software	31	42	56, 59	76, 80	98	104, 106, 108
Communicating information	CD-ROM			56	74, 83		
Communicating information	Authoring software	28, 31	46		83	92	106
Communicating information	Notation software			65			110, 114
Communicating information	Music software	26, 34	46	59, 65, 68	78, 80, 83	94, 96	106, 114
Control	Tape recorder		42				
Monitoring	Microphone	31					
Communicating information/Control	Keyboard/MIDI interface	26, 31, 34	46	52, 65, 68	86	94	110, 114

SOFTWARE TYPE	BBC/MASTER	RISCOS	NIMBUS/186	WINDOWS	MACINTOSH
Word processor	Pendown Folio	Pendown Desk Top Folio	All Write Write On	Word for Windows Kid Works 2 Creative Writer	Kid Works 2 Easy Works Creative Writer
Art package	Image	1st Paint Kid Pix Splash	PaintSpa	Colour Magic Kid Pix 2 Fine Artist	Kid Pix 2 Flying Colours Fine Artist
Drawing software		Draw Vector Art Works		Claris Works Oak Draw	Claris Works
Multi-media authoring		Magpie Hyperstudio Genesis		Genesis Hyperstudio Illuminus	Hyperstudio
Music	Compose	Compose World Music Box Music Maker	Compose	Music Box Music Explorer Music Maker	Thinkin things Toony Loons
Notation		Notate Rhapsody			

	ENGLISH	MATHS	SCIENCE	HISTORY	GEOGRAPHY	ART	TECHNOLOGY	PE	RE
BASIC SKILLS		Counting in sets.	Investigating sounds.				Making own scales from tubing etc.	Using movement up and down.	
COMPOSING	Using poetry.	Probability (dice); nets and cubes; counting in sets.	Investigating how sounds are made; sound pictures to represent scientific themes e.g. space/ plants, forces, electricity.	Sound pictures of: Hadrian's Wall and roads; also other historical themes.	Sound pictures of: Roman construction; land use; roads; river journey; landforms e.g. mountains, volcanoes.	Impressionism; representing colour with music e.g. warm or cold colours; pictures as stimulus.	Making dice (sets); machine compositions, actions and body sounds/ instruments.	Composing music for movement and dance.	Composing music for rituals and ceremonies.
LISTENING	Writing in variety of styles; developing vocabulary; describing music.	Data handling ('graph').	How do you hear sound? How the ear works.	Home entertainments e.g. Tudors listening to viol consorts and Victorians to piano playing.	Listening in different parts of world/cultures: listening as a whole experience using movement, breathing, thinking, doing.	Using abstract pattern to represent sound; exploring different medium; collage to represent sound.	Technology of listening: HiFi, Ghetto blasters; compare to find the best system.	Creating folk dances in response to music.	Listening as a form of prayer or meditation.
CLASSICAL MUSIC	Use of Tudor language; use of story; describing music.	Data handling ('graph'); use of grid notation; counting beats; counting in 3s.	Electronic contemporary music.	Tudor court life; instruments in 17th and 18th century; Victorian social life.	*Fingal's Cave* (Mendelssohn) *Vltava* (Smetna) Pastoral Symphony (Beethoven)	Links with Baroque architecture and minimalism in art.	John Cage, Arvo Pärt; everyday objects and toys in music eg. squeaky ducks.	Links with dance (ballet and waltz).	History of sacred music in Western cultures: Byrd, Bach, Handel.
WORLD MUSIC	Awareness of language through songs of different cultures.	Intervals: 4ths; counting in sets; prime numbers; common denominators; data handling ('graph').	How sound is made by instruments from different parts of the world.	Reference to Crusades and Tudor instruments; history of slave trade.	North Africa; West Africa; China; South-East Asia (Java); India; British Isles culture.	Muslim art and architecture; integration of music, art and dance in different cultures.	How to make a… digeridoo, panpipes; how instruments are made in different cultures.	Use of world music for dance.	Reference to dragon dance (festivals); music for a religious theme.
POP, ROCK AND JAZZ	Writing reports; writing song words; rhythm and style of language.	Counting in sets.	Science of electronic instruments; digitally sampled sound.	Traditional music; history of popular music.	Movement of music and culture across the world e.g. slave trade, spirituals.	Using pop-art style.	Unconventional use of everyday objects.	Disco dancing.	Gospel singing; spirituals.
NOTATION	Use of signs and symbols; understanding different signs and symbols to represent music.	Data handling (grids); simple computation; counting in sets.	Notating and drawing sound waves.	History of notation of music: medieval, Tudor, stave, contemporary, graphic.	Notation in different parts of the world.	Using symbols and colour to represent sounds.	Notation represented on solid shapes, spirals, cones etc.	Using children to represent notation e.g. each child represents a note/sound.	Illuminated manuscrips of early sacred music.